Washington Women as Path Breakers

Northwest Native American women, including this Makah mother and daughter, wove sturdy baskets in which they gathered and stored food. They tossed heated rocks into tightly-woven baskets to boil food. When settlers brought iron pots and other goods, Indian women were eager to use them. Having little access to money, they wove smaller, decorative baskets which they traded and sold, contributing substantially to their tribes' economies. Photo by Samuel G. Morse. (Courtesy of the Washington State Historical Society, Tacoma, Photo #502)

Washington Women as Path Breakers

Mildred Tanner Andrews

Sponsored by the Junior League of Tacoma

KENDALL/HUNT PUBLISHING COMPANY
2460 Kerper Boulevard P.O. Box 539 Dubuque, Iowa 52004-0539

Copyright © 1989 by Junior League of Tacoma

Library of Congress Catalog Card Number: 88-84070

ISBN 0–8403–5215–8

Printed in the United States of America
10 9 8 7 6 5 4 3 2 1

This book, the companion curriculum guide for teachers,
and a travelling photographic exhibit
were made possible by grants from the following:

MAJOR DONORS

The 1989 Washington Centennial Commission

The Murray Foundation in Memory of Helen Bailey Murray

The Medina Foundation

$2,000–$2,500

The Norcliffe Fund

$1,000–$2,000

Ruth A. Wheeler
in Memory of Mr. and Mrs. R. E. Anderson
and
Mr. and Mrs. Welles Wheeler,
Parents of Ruth and Henry Wheeler

The Skinner Foundation

The Washington Commission for the Humanities, a Non-profit
Organization Supported by the National Endowment for the
Humanities and by Private Contributors

$500–$1,000

His Family in Memory of James H. Clapp

Dorothy Simpson in Honor of the Founders of Seattle
Junior Programs

The Ladies' Aid Society of Spokane's First Congregational Church, organized in 1879 in the home of the Rev. Henry Thomas Cowley and his wife Lucy Abigail Peet Cowley (seated, right). The ladies held an annual Apple Blossom Tea when the trees on the Cowley place were in bloom. They continue to observe the tradition today. (Courtesy Margaret Paine Cowles)

Contents

In two expeditions, Asa Mercer brought more than 40 unmarried women from New England to Seattle. Although Mercer discreetly enticed the women with promises of job opportunities, it was obvious to most of them that he was seeking a partial solution to Washington's "bachelor problem" of the 1860s. All but one of the "Mercer Girls" eventually married, enriching Puget Sound families with the culture and education that they had brought with them from their native New England. Drawing from *Harper's Weekly,* January, 1866. (Special Collections Div., Univ. of Washington Libraries, A. C. Warner Photo #68)

Japanese proxy brides arrive in Seattle, seeking to recognize their betrothed. Lonely men from Germany, Greece, Japan and other countries wrote to their families back home to enlist help in finding a wife. When agreement was reached, the young woman would leave her home with a one-way ticket and the man's photograph in hand. Occasionally, a man deceived his bride by sending the wrong picture or by claiming to be wealthy when he was poor, but in many cases a good marriage was the result. (Courtesy of the Japanese American Citizens League, Seattle)

Foreword

I am delighted to introduce this substantial contribution to our understanding of Washington State's history. In this fascinating book, Mildred Andrews brings to light a part of our history that has not been told.

Through a rich array of archival photographs and lively narrative, the book tells about the women who founded libraries, schools, hospitals, arts institutes, parks, museums, service agencies and more. It also sheds light on women's political activities and how they have influenced the development of our communities and our state.

With this publication, the Junior League of Tacoma honors the many women whose caring and commitment have helped to build our state's heritage. It is a part of our history to which all of us can relate and I see it as a source of inspiration for the future.

Jean Gardner
First Lady, Washington State
Co-chair, Washington State Centennial Commission

(Courtesy of Washington State Centennial Commission)

This eastern Washington woman could be on her way to a women's club, church guild, temperance society, or suffrage meeting. (Courtesy of the Eastern Washington State Historical Society, Spokane, Photo #L84–423.22.2)

Preface and Acknowledgments

Eliminate the valleys from the landscape and the mountains will float surrealistically in the sky, disconnected from the earth. Eliminate women and families and the dailyness of life from history and what remains is a distorted portrait of the past.

The metaphor, "path breakers," conjures up images of adventurous explorers, military leaders, statesmen and builders of business empires—the pantheon of traditional Washington State history. With a few notable exceptions (pioneer missionary, Narcissa Whitman; Nellie Cornish, founder of an arts institute; Mother Joseph, the Northwest's first architect; and Lewis and Clark guide, Sacajewea), women are not included. My purpose in writing this history is to bring to light previously obscured paths of women who from Washington's earliest history to the present have joined together in a collective crusade to enrich the quality of life for themselves and those around them.

Through their voluntary associations, Washington women of all races, creeds, and economic strata have traditionally organized and acted to provide needed services and to nurture cultural enrichment in their communities. Early suffragists, temperance workers and clubwomen, like contemporary feminists, worked together to lobby for "women's issues," such as equal rights, child care, support for public education, and equal pay for work of equal value (now called "comparable worth"). This book explores the ebb and flow of the "women's movement," which, when politically strong, has effectively impacted state and federal law. Its foundation, however, is an unbroken stream made up of women's ongoing voluntary commitments.

In recent years, historians have begun to address omissions in western and women's history. In the early 1980s, the Washington Women's Heritage Project produced a statewide photographic exhibit and slide show with the theme, "Sharing and Caring." The project was a pilot in grassroots history, which gave impetus to an effort to collect women's diaries, personal correspondence, scrapbooks, club records and oral history interviews. As a result, many of our state's libraries and historical societies are building collections of materials that were previously considered unimportant and unworthy of preservation. The acquisitions are creating a needed data base to enable historians to begin to sort out the past as it relates to women. Other recent statewide historical projects on Washington women deal with specific ethnic groups or specific orientations, such as judges, legislators, and artists. At the local level, there have been women's history conferences, celebrations, and displays to commemorate the contributions of women to their communities.

Washington Women as Path Breakers is the first book to take a more general and inclusive approach. By focusing on women's roles as creators of more livable communities and as agents of change, I have attempted to build a comprehensive framework to give perspective and context to other more specific projects. This is both a social history and a non-partisan political history, designed to foster a multidimensional interpretation of the past to which families, children, volunteers and all members of our communities can relate. Although my major emphasis is on the period between 1870 and 1940, I make frequent connections to the region's ancient Native American heritage and to its early settlers. Similarly, there are numerous examples that extend into the present and lead toward the future.

The immediate prototype for this book was my illustrated history, *Seattle Women: a Legacy of Community Development,* published in 1984 by the Seattle/King County YWCA. Since that time, I have been asked to give presentations not only in Seattle, but in cities throughout Washington and in other western states. Everywhere, people have been able to recognize a related legacy among women in their own communities. Children delight in stories of the early PTA which for them validate the contributions of their own parents. Adults, who are almost always surprised by the extent of women's contributions, gain a new appreciation for their female forebears and for the value of voluntarism. Historians find grist for questions that they ponder, such as whether the frontier was a liberating experience for women. Doubtless, Victorian idealism accompanied women to the frontier. As fast as they could, western women organized clubs, church guilds, and other modicums of the "society" that they had known elsewhere. Nonetheless, in their upheaval and in the exigencies of their new environment, women in the Northwest voted long before their eastern sisters.

With the Washington State Centennial Celebration at hand, women from all over the state have asked me to expand my study of Seattle women to a statewide perspective. Many view the Centennial with its immense array of state and local events as a golden opportunity to escalate the process of restoring women to their proper place in history. My work will hopefully serve as a stimulus to infuse women's legacy into other historical projects throughout the state.

Washington Women as Path Breakers has been an enormous challenge, one that I could never have undertaken without considerable assistance. In the tradition of women's organizations, it is the result of extensive collaboration. I am grateful, first of all, to the Junior League of Tacoma whose members, on the recommendation of then president Linda Robson, voted to sponsor this project three years ago as their contribution to our State Centennial Celebration.

I was further heartened by endorsements and letters of support from the following: the American Association of University Women, Washington State Division; the Washington State Coalition of Labor Union Women; the Washington State Federation of Business and Professional Women; Washington Women United; the Washington State Women's Political Caucus; the Office of the Washington State Superintendent of Public Instruction; Susan Armitage, Director, American Studies Program, Washington State University; Karen Blair, Assistant Professor, History, Central Washington University; and Esther Mumford, past President, Black Heritage Society of Washington State.

I could not possibly name all of the people who have shared insights, information and records with me during the past eight years to help shape my interpretation of Washington women's history. Some influenced my perceptions through lengthy interviews and written correspondence; on other occasions a casual conversation helped clarify my ideas. There are several individuals to whom I owe a special "thank you."

I greatly appreciate the assistance of the many archivists, librarians, and curators of special collections who burrowed through their collections to help me find elusive records of women and who guided me in my selection of photographs. Among them are: Richard Engeman, Curator of Photographs, and other staff, University of Washington Libraries' Special Collections Division; Karyl Winn and her staff, University of Washington's Manuscripts Collection; Carolyn Marr and Rick Caldwell, Seattle's Museum of History and Industry; Eleanor Toews, Seattle Public Schools Archives; Elaine Miller, Washington State Historical Society, Tacoma; Ed Nolan, Eastern Washington State Historical Society, Spokane; Susan Edmonds and Lynne Hollingsworth, Western Washington University Library; Cindy Richardson, Western Washington University Music Library; Nancy Compau, Spokane Public Library; James Scott, Center for Pacific Northwest Studies in Bellingham; Lawrence Dodd, Northwest and Whitman College Archives; Ross Rieder, Pacific Northwest Labor History Association; Nell Ranta, Coalition of Labor Union Women; Jean Gillmer, Tacoma Public Library; Carolyn Willberg, Ellensburg Public Library; Gayle Palmer and Jeanne Engerman, Washington State Library, Olympia; Eunice Darvill, Skagit County Historical Museum; Dorothy Cordova, Demonstration Project for Asian Americans; Margaret Riddle, Everett Public Library; Sister Rita Bergamini and Loretta Greene, Sisters of Providence Archives; Mary Rouse, Newcastle Historical Society; Cecelia Kayano and Norma Raver, Pacific Peaks Girl Scout Council; Edward and Elizabeth Burke, Nippon Kan Heritage Association; Sylvia Meyer, Washington Children's Home Society; Ronald Fields, Chairman, Art Department, University of Puget Sound; Sid White, Director, Peoples of Washington Project; Pat Matheny White, Chicano Archives, the Evergreen State College; Gail Nomura, Director, Asian/Pacific American Studies Program at Washington State University and Project Director, Japanese American Pioneers in the Yakima Valley Photo Exhibit; Richard Major, Croatian Fraternal Union of America; Charles Peyton, Association of King County Historical Organizations; Kathryn Hinsch, Project Director of "Political Pioneers, a Study of Women in the Washington State Legislature;" Carole Reddaway and Betty Stadum, Seattle/King County Council of Camp Fire; Gloria Martin, Shakespeare and Martin bookstore; Barbara Krohn, Women in Communications, Inc.; and Colleen Cavanagh, Annie Wright School.

Numerous others have shared their insights, photographs, records and referrals. I sincerely appreciate the help of Ruth Anderson Wheeler, Lowell Butson, Amy Lou Young, Eugenia Currie, Willard Jue (deceased), Priscilla Chong Jue, Louise Hwang Yook, Paul Dorpat, Margaret Paine Cowles, Marina Pavlovna Reva Dietsch, Roger Barron, Ella Aquino (deceased), Frances Penrose Owen, Kay Bullitt, Ann Wyckoff, Nancy Skinner Nordhoff, Sally Skinner Behnke, Dorothy Simpson, Winifred Weter, Marion Fish Cox (deceased), Bertha Pitts Campbell, Jeanette Edris Rockefeller,

Evelyn Sun, Kay Bullitt, Patsy Bullitt Collins, Anne Farrell, Judge Evangeline Starr, State Representative Jennifer Belcher, Rosanne Gostovich Royer, Jean Smith Sherar, Ann Harder McKenzie Wyatt, Patria Robinson Martin, Pam Clapp, Lindy Cater, Suzanne Pate, Earlyse Allen Swift, Irene Wentworth, Paul Pitzer, Jennifer James-Wilson, and Brenda Owings-Klimek.

My very special thanks to Linda Smith, Susan Armitage, Nancy Compau and Judy Robinette, each of whom read all or parts of the manuscript and helped me to clarify my thoughts. As all of them know, many of the conclusions in this book are my own, based on the above formal and informal research. In the process, we have had some stimulating conversations, comparing what I have shown with their additional resources and insights. I invite the reader to join in the fun of discussing, debating, and exploring the contributions of women to Washington State's history.

Finally, members of my own family have given me a special kind of support that could come from nowhere else. My mother, Mildred Chargois Tanner (a third generation Washingtonian, who now makes her home in Coeur d'Alene, Idaho), has been a constant source of moral support. My husband, George, has been the best of companions, giving me encouragement to bolster my energy, whenever it lagged. As in the past, he has read the manuscript prior to anyone else and has helped to keep me on track. This book is for them.

The Rev. David E. and Catherine Payne Blaine. Seattle's first private school teacher was one of the original American suffragists who in 1848 signed the Declaration of the Rights of Women at Seneca Falls, New York. Parents of 13 girls and one boy paid tuition so that their children could attend her school from Tuesday through Saturday. Mrs. Blaine reserved Sunday for church and Monday for her washing. (Courtesy of Special Collections Div., Univ. of Washington Archives, UW Neg. #1866)

Introduction

Abigail Scott Duniway, the Northwest's leading suffragist, threw down the gauntlet for future historians in 1914, when she wrote *Path Breaking: an Autobiographical History of the Equal Suffrage Movement in Pacific Coast States*. Her book inspired the title of this one and her challenge has had an influence on its contents.

A covered-wagon pioneer, the 17-year-old Duniway had helped bury her mother on the trail before arriving in Oregon in 1852. She married a man who promised to protect and care for her, but like many other western women, she discovered that the anticipated "passive" role of wife and mother was not to be hers. Due to financial reversals, her husband lost his farm and then suffered an accident that incapacitated him for life. With six children and an infirm spouse, the self-educated Duniway left the rugged farm life to move to town and assume the responsibility of supporting her family.

Her harsh experiences had ripped away the veil of illusion that still enshrouded women as the weaker, inferior sex and that denied them full citizenship. Channeling her enormous energy to the cause of equal suffrage, Duniway founded, edited and wrote her own newspaper, *The New Northwest,* as a voice for the movement. In Washington, she ventured by stagecoach and steamboat throughout the territory to reach communities large and small. An eloquent and witty orator, she championed her cause while raising public consciousness about courageous, struggling women whose shared mission was to civilize the rough-hewn frontier. During her long lifetime, Duniway saw the northwestern states become the nation's first stronghold of women's suffrage. Her story is pure American and pure frontier as she breaks new paths, trying to open the way to women's participation as full and equal partners in society.

At the end of her autobiography, she admonishes young college women to remember that their freedom to go to school and to choose their occupation "was bought for them at a great price." She says, "It is for them to show their gratitude by helping onward the reforms of their own time, . . . The debt that each generation owes to the past it must pay to the future."[1]

Duniway's challenge to historians is to illuminate the past and make it relevant on a human scale. So that contemporary generations can pay their debt to the future, they must know what they owe the past. Susan Armitage, Director of American Studies at Washington State University, echoes Duniway's challenge, while simultaneously suggesting guidelines for meeting it. She takes exception to traditional histories of the American West which focus on grand events and superhuman heroes. She says, "There is another story of the Northwest, the story of new beginnings, of daily life, community-building, the development of local and regional networks and organizations, the growth of the sense of regional identity and distinctiveness. That story—one is tempted to say, the real story—cannot be written without women, for they were full participants in those events."[2]

When traditional historians, folklorists, and romanticizers of the wild West include women, they generally present a one-dimensional, distorted image. Among legendary stereotypes are the sunbonneted farm wife, the beleaguered dancehall girl, the tight-lipped temperance worker and the straight-laced schoolmarm. Like cardboard props in a stage set, these images fade into the background with little or no character development. Susan Armitage discusses another group of stereotyped western women, namely the "gentle tamers." "Their very presence on the frontier was enough to make rough and rowdy men think about polite behavior and the establishment of civilized institutions like schools, churches, libraries and the rest. What's striking about this stereotype is the unbelievable passivity of the women. Women didn't have to *do* anything: they simply had to be there and men would build communities around them."[3] This book strips away the masks from the above stereotypes, while dispelling the myth of passive, idyllic women. This is the story of women who both individually and collectively acted out their parts and took responsibility for their lives.

Washington State is an excellent place to begin to unfold "the real story" of western history because of the lateness of its settlement. Historical records, photographs and stories handed down from pioneer grandmothers still remain in tact. Native Americans, whose history dates back thousands of years, have preserved much of their past through the oral tradition of story-telling. Another factor that makes Washington especially interesting is its immense diversity. Topographically, the state commands multifarious life styles with families making their homes in logging and mining communities, on farms, in fishing villages, in small towns and in bustling cities. Demographically, Washington has benefited from numerous immigrations, making its population one of the most ethnically diverse in the country.

The region's first women pioneers were Protestant missionary wives: Narcissa Whitman at Waiilatpu (near Walla Walla); Eliza Spaulding at Lapwai (now on the Nez Perce Reservation in Idaho, just east of Clarkston); and Myra Eells and Mary Richardson Walker at Tshimakain (near Kettle Falls). Like other women who followed, they banded together to form an organization to provide mutual support. The Columbia Maternal Association was a unique type of sisterhood. At a prescribed hour each day, each woman at her own isolated mission went off alone to pray, meditate, and think of herself and her sisters. When on infrequent occasions the women saw each other, they felt united.

As Washington's population grew, it quickly gained multicultural, multilingual, and multiracial dimensions. In 1855, the United States government, represented by Governor Isaac Stevens, made its first treaty with Native Americans in the Washington Territory. Stevens arranged to pay $15,000 in 20 annual installments for most of what later became King, Snohomish, Whatcom, Island, Kitsap and Skagit Counties. In accord with the treaty, the tribes kept 48,000 acres of reservation lands to which they reluctantly moved. By the 1850s, there were black women and families in the territory, followed by successive waves of Asian and European immigrants. Among the first to become established were German and Polish Jews who by the 1870s constituted a thriving ethnic community in Walla Walla.

In pioneer society, men far outnumbered women, frequently coming alone to seek their fortune as laborers, fishermen, lumbermen, merchants, or seafarers. Be they American or foreign born, women often waited at home until their husbands, fathers or betrothed could afford to send for them. For the first women of any group, life was especially difficult, since most were expected to care for their families along with their husband's bachelor relatives and friends.

With courage and ingenuity, women pioneers struggled against hardship to create comfortable homes for themselves and their families. It was primarily through the family unit that they began to undergird the social structure of their new communities. By gradually incorporating old and new values, they exerted a stabilizing influence, creating a sense of pride, belonging and hope for themselves and their loved ones. While men tended to business and politics, women soon joined together to form their own organizations, which for them were a means of exerting a collective influence on their communities.

Most Washington women worked as mothers, teachers, nurses, seamstresses, salesclerks, housekeepers, and farm laborers. A few enjoyed professional status as doctors, lawyers, professors, dentists, business managers and school superintendents. Some gave music lessons. Others did whatever had to be done in family businesses. Some took in laundry, sold home-churned butter and eggs, or cared for neighbors' children. Still others were fortunate enough to belong to the leisure class. Yet most, married or single, professional or working class, found time and energy for complex lives that included family, work and a wide range of community organizations, ranging from sophisticated clubs to informal "neighbor helping neighbor" networks.

Whether they claimed to be political or non-political, early Washington women's organizations generally shared a common goal which was to improve the quality of life in their communities. This book unfolds the story of their quest for social reform and for equal rights. It also brings to light their legacy as founders of institutions, services and amenities that many of us take for granted today. Traditional histories have generally ignored their contributions, but they deserve to be recalled.

Notes

1. Abigail Scott Duniway, *Path Breaking: an Autobiographical History of the Equal Suffrage Movement in Pacific Coast States* with New Introduction by Eleanor Flexner, Reprinted from the James, Kerns & Abbott edition of 1914 (New York: Schocken Books, 1914), p. 297.
2. Susan Armitage, "Western Women: Beginning to Come into Focus," *Montana: the Magazine of Western History,* Summer 1982, pp. 2–9.
3. Ibid.

Washington Women as Path Breakers

Canoe racing was a popular athletic event for coastal Native Americans. The Makah hosted 4th of July contests at Neah Bay, where this crew of women (ca. 1900) prepares for a race against women from Klallam, La Push, and Vancouver Island. At a time when Indian agents did their best to obliterate the traditional culture, tribal Elders strove to keep it alive for younger generations. The American Independence Day was an excellent pretext for holding their own time-honored celebrations. Photo by Samuel G. Morse. (Courtesy of the Washington State Historical Society, Morse #100)

The Suffrage Crusade

1

As newly elected president of the General Federation of Women's Clubs, Sarah Platt Decker of Denver addressed the 1904 convention in an eloquent appeal for club women to become involved in social issues. She said, "Ladies, you have chosen me your leader. Well, I have an important piece of news to give you. Dante is dead. He has been dead for several centuries, and I think it is time that we dropped the study of his Inferno and turned our attention to our own."[1]

Her message added fuel to a fire that had already flamed for years in many of the clubs and in national organizations such as the Women's Christian Temperance Union, women's suffrage associations, and consumer leagues, all of which were concerned with changing America's priorities to focus on human welfare and on more livable communities. Nowhere was the movement more alive than in the Washington Territory, where the founding of the first women's clubs in the 1880s coincided with a temporarily victorious suffrage campaign.

The Franchise—Won and Lost

The struggle for women's enfranchisement had begun at the first session of the Territorial Legislature in 1854, when Seattle's founder, Arthur Armstrong Denny, proposed a bill to grant the ballot to white women. Some surmised that the motion lost because at least one dissenting lawmaker was married to a Native American. Later, when election codes were rewritten to include "all white citizens," the legislators repeatedly voted down proposals to concede that women were citizens.

It was an issue that resounded throughout the nation. Early suffragists, led by Susan B. Anthony and Elizabeth Cady Stanton had raised their voices as avowed abolitionists. They assumed that the passage of the 14th and 15th Amendments to the United States Constitution, intended to enfranchise black men, would logically pave the way for women's suffrage. Section one of the 14th Amendment, which was ratified in 1868, defined "all persons born or naturalized in the United States" as citizens. To the suffragists' amazement, section two used the word "male" to modify "citizen" for the first time anywhere in the Constitution.

Left to right: unknown, Susan B. Anthony, Abigail Scott Duniway, Elizabeth Cady Stanton, unknown. Ca. 1890, somewhere in the East. (Courtesy of Special Collections Div., Univ. of Washington Libraries, UW Neg. #9168)

Some respectable women decided to test the definition and claim their rights as citizens. When Mary Olney Brown tried to vote in Olympia, she was refused. However, her sister, Mary Olney Smith, and a group of other women in Grand Mound successfully cast their ballots.

Anthony and Stanton embarked on a nationwide tour to promote their cause. Among those who made a fervent commitment to help was Oregon's Abigail Scott Duniway. At her invitation, the 50-year-old Anthony joined her on a 10-week, 2,000-mile lecture tour through the rugged Pacific Northwest.

Inspired by their visit in 1871, supportive women and men met in Olympia to organize the Washington Women Suffrage Association. At the same time, an editorial in the *Washington Standard* questioned the wisdom of abolishing women's "social and domestic supremacy:" ". . . would their [women's] own happiness and the good order, morality and refinement of society be promoted by removing the conventional barriers heretofore dividing the sexes? Could women afford to surrender the prerogatives and special privileges conceded them by social privilege in enlightened communities for the questionable privilege of sharing with men in the turmoil and strife of political elections?"[2]

Nonetheless, as the temperance crusade swept the nation, the Good Templars, Protestant churches, and other involved organizations joined forces with suffragists, seeing the women's vote as a means of implementing reform. In Washington, the collaboration proved costly, since a powerful saloon lobby held sway over legislators who repeatedly voted down bills to enfranchise women.

In a calculated move that affronted many of her co-workers, Duniway determined that suffrage and prohibition should be treated as separate issues. She saw the former as an inalienable right and the latter as a process of education and reform. In Washington, where men outnumbered women seven to one, she feared imperiling suffrage by wielding it as a prohibitionist's club.

In the tradition of the first generation suffragists, she cited the 14th and 15th Amendments, arguing that women's equality should be the next step in the democratization of America. As the Northwest's leading suffragist, she traveled by stagecoach, steamboat, and horseback to communities in all parts of Washington and neighboring territories. She lobbied, lectured, and gathered stories which she published in her pro-suffrage tabloid, the *New Northwest*.

Possibly because of Duniway's change in tactics, Washington in 1883 became the third territory in the nation to enfranchise women, preceded only by Wyoming and Utah. The victory, however, was short-lived. Ignoring Duniway's protestations, the new voters zealously set forth to wield their power against vice and the demon rum.

Sarah Yesler, clothed and coifed in the style of the 1870s, attended Washington's first suffrage meeting in Olympia and then went home to head the Seattle association. (Courtesy of Special Collections Div., Univ. of Washington Libraries, UW Neg. #2439)

Lucy B. Thomas recalled the situation in rural Yakima, where mothers had done their best to entertain young people in their homes and to keep them "going straight." With the vote, they determined to put the town's saloons, brothels, and gambling dens—profitable sources of revenue to their owners and to local government—out of business.

Church women donned their white ribbons of temperance to organize a strenuous campaign. At the subsequent local election, prohibition won and the town of Yakima was legally dry. A skeptical Thomas saw the handwriting on the wall and predicted that she and her sisters would not have their way for long. "The men said if we didn't have any better sense than to vote for prohibition, we didn't have enough sense to vote at all."[3]

Charles J. Woodbury, who was traveling through Washington, wrote his observations to the New York *Evening Post:* "Whatever may be the vicissitudes of women suffrage in Washington Territory in the future, it should now be put on record that at the election, November 4, 1884, nine-tenths of its adult female population availed themselves of the right to vote with a hearty enthusiasm."

Later in his letter, Woodbury commented on his visit to Seattle where the women's vote had tipped the balance for proponents of law and order: "Even the bars of the hotels were closed; and this was the worst town in the territory when I first saw it. Now its uproarious theaters, dance-houses, squaw brothels [which employed Native American women] and Sunday fights are things of the past. Not a gambling house exists."

Seattle weathered its purity for only a year. As loggers and miners squandered their paychecks in more liberal communities, the city coffers diminished. At the next election voters threw law and order proponents out of office; they repealed anti-vice laws and welcomed back the madams, pimps, saloon-keepers and other fun-loving purveyors of iniquity. As in the past, fines and licenses for liquor, gambling and prostitution were the major source of revenue for city government.

Echoing Duniway's admonitions, the tide quickly turned against women's enfranchisement. Within four years of its passage, the Territorial Supreme Court bowed to pressure from the saloon lobby and declared the suffrage law invalid, basing its decision on a technicality. In 1889, when Washington men voted to ratify the state constitution, they defeated a proposed equal suffrage amendment by a margin of more than two to one. The State Legislature then restored women's right to vote in school elections.

5

Tacoma's Nesika Club, 1894. Founder, Virginia Mason, is in the center of the top row. (Courtesy of the Washington State Historical Society, #40)

Not everyone wanted equal rights. These Spokane women, aboard the toboggan, probably would not have wanted to trade places with architect Kirtland Cutter and pals, who strain to pull them up Howard Street. (Courtesy of the Spokane Public Library, Northwest Room)

From Organization to Agitation

Despite their loss of social and legal equality, women had made significant strides during their brief period of enfranchisement. With the exception of church guilds, there had been very few women's organizations during the early suffrage campaign. In 1883, when the transcontinental railroad reached its terminus in Tacoma, it heralded a population explosion that included educated women who had already participated in cultural and service organizations in the East and who were eager to help found them in their new communities.

The Club Movement

Members of national associations, including the PEO (a sorority dedicated to education), the Order of the Eastern Star (the women's affiliate of the Masons), and others began to establish local chapters. As national president of the well-organized Women's Christian Temperance Union,

Frances Willard took her first look at the territory's topography and declared that Washington should have two unions—one east and one west of the craggy Cascade Mountains. Local units burgeoned in communities large and small with strong regional support and a clear mission to bring about social reform through advocacy, education and service.

The territory's first women's club was organized in Olympia when a group of 11 women elected Abigail H. H. Stuart (former head of the city's suffrage association) as president. The idea quickly caught fire with similar clubs blossoming all over Washington as fast as women could organize them. Earlier in the century with the rise of industrialization, women in the East had taken the initially radical step of founding social, literary and self-improvement clubs that drew them away from their homemaking spheres. Austensibly, the clubs nurtured the Victorian "cult of true womanhood," which extolled the virtues of piety, purity, domesticity and submissiveness.

The Woman's Social Club for Mutual Improvement (later renamed the Woman's Club of Olympia) had similar beginnings. In keeping with their domestic priorities, clubwomen soon began to view their communities as an extension of their homes, realizing that in sisterhood, they could embark on a nurturing, civilizing mission. As a result, many of the clubs, including the one in Olympia, expanded their agenda to include human services and advocacy for more livable communities—programs that they called "social housekeeping." (Similar activities undertaken by men were labeled "progressive reform.")

In 1890, the Olympia group became a charter member of the General Federation of Women's Clubs. Six years later, Tacoma's Nesika and Aloha Clubs called a convention to organize the Washington State Federation of Women's Clubs. Women who were excluded from the predominantly white, middle-class GFWC banded together to form similar associations of their own. There were local chapters of the National Council of Jewish Women, the Daughters of Norway, the Vasa Lodge, the Fidelia Club for Italian women and the Japanese Methodist Girls' Club. Black women's clubs met in Spokane to organize the Colored Women's Federation of Washington. In Tacoma, the Slavonian Women's Lodge hosted gatherings that drew families from as far away as Bellingham and Portland.

Other women organized along professional lines with statewide associations of nurses, teachers, and physicians. Waitresses and garment workers formed their own unions. In rural areas, women participated in the Grange, where they enjoyed the right to vote and hold office. On their reservations,

Giving a literal interpretation to "municipal housekeeping," Tacoma's Methodist Episcopal Broom Brigade staged performances to raise funds for church pews and other furnishings. 1884. (Courtesy of the Washington State Historical Society, #48)

8

Bellingham's Aftermath Club built this elegant clubhouse in 1905. Today, the facility continues to host banquets, conventions, weddings, dances, and meetings. (Courtesy of the Center for Pacific Northwest Studies)

Native American women were harassed by government agents who were determined to stamp out their language and cultural heritage. The women, who had long served on tribal councils, as medicine women and sometimes as chiefs, kept alive the ancient teachings to preserve them for younger generations.

Women's Cooperative Societies

Following the economic panic of 1893, Frances C. Axtell was elected president of the New Whatcom Ladies' Cooperative Society, which aimed to help people of all classes "enjoy a greater degree of prosperity and happiness." With a membership of about 500, the ladies worked to establish the flax industry, their city's first creamery, public playgrounds, and more.

The New Whatcom group soon took a leadership role in forming the Women's Washington State Cooperative Society whose slogan was "Patronize Home Industry." In recessionary periods, including the later Great Depression of the 1930s, the society was a mainstay, intensively promoting the patronage of local enterprise and setting up soup kitchens for the unemployed and their families.

Another example of women's economic activity was in Spokane, where in 1898, club women raised the final $15,000 to bring Fort George Wright to their city. Caught in a financial crisis, city fathers had secured the required land donation, but were stymied for the hard cash. Business woman, Alice Houghton, called on her club sisters to come to the rescue. The women sparked public enthusiasm, getting citizens to contribute whatever they could for prizes and selling dollar tickets for a massive raffle at the "Fort

Members of Seattle's Japanese Methodist Episcopal Mission provided needed services to their community. In addition to their church work, women worked in family businesses, such as laundry and farming. They often had to care for extended families, including their husbands' bachelor friends for whom they sewed, did laundry, and cooked. This undated photograph is presumably early, since by the 1900s, many of the women were adopting western dress. (Courtesy of Special Collections Div., Univ. of Washington Libraries, UW Neg. #416)

Jennie Shaw Wheeler supported herself in local agricultural enterprises which were aggressively promoted by women's Cooperative Societies. She sold her weight in spices to buy a bicycle in Hoquiam in 1899, then married and moved to White Bluffs on the Columbia where she packed boxes of fruit. Heartbreak came in 1943, when the government took over the entire community for Hanford. Without even being able to wait for harvest, the family moved to Tacoma. (Washington Women's Heritage Project Records, University of Washington Libraries)

Christmas Tree." Donated prizes ran the gamut from gold watches to pickles, music lessons, a cow, electric baths, surgical and dental work, chewing tobacco, mince meat pies, and more.

Thanks to Spokane clubwomen, Fort Wright came to the city, along with thousands of soldiers whose paychecks bolstered the local economy. In what may have become a branch of the Women's Washington State Cooperative Society, Spokane women perpetuated their efforts through a new organization called "Nemow Enakops" (to be read backwards). Every member vowed to use products made in Spokane, to assist in establishing industries, and to do what they could to increase the population and beautify the city.

Political Orientation

Through their organizations, Washington women were learning the political skills of parliamentary procedure, public speaking, conventioneering, fundraising, and networking to implement their programs and to bring about social reform. Long before they could vote, women lobbied successfully for passage of pure food laws, for allocations to support public libraries, against billboards, for better pay and conditions for working women, and for adding home economies and manual arts to the public school curriculum.

Although the GFWC, according to its charter was not political, its leaders publicly touted the influence of club women on almost every state legislature. Like the WCTU, which from its inception had had a political orientation, the clubs were primed for non-partisan political action, ready to take on reforms and causes in which they believed.

Laundry workers, such as this multi-racial group, were among the first women's labor unions. They joined the Washington State Federation of Labor, which gave it strong endorsement to suffrage. (Courtesy of the Tacoma Public Library)

Big yellow posters went out with each issue of "Votes for Women," a Washington suffrage campaign tabloid. Subscribers all over the state were bound by their loyalty to the cause to post them in conspicuous spots. (Courtesy of Special Collections Div., Univ. of Washington Libraries, Asahel Curtis #19943)

The Franchise Regained

Buoyed by fervent turn-of-the-century reform movements, Washington women tackled the suffrage issue with renewed vigor, determined once and for all to regain the franchise. A key player was Emma Smith DeVoe, a poised, lady-like, seasoned organizer for the National American Women's Suffrage Association, who moved to Tacoma in 1906 to be elected president of the Washington Equal Suffrage Association. For the next two years, she travelled constantly to communities all over the state, meticulously organizing a campaign.

Among her co-workers were Ellen Swinburg Leckenby and Dr. Cora Smith Eaton of Seattle, who at first contributed part of her office for WESA headquarters. Carrie Chapman Catt, founder of Seattle's Women's Century Club and a leading national suffragist, was involved, as was Oregon's Abigail Scott Duniway. One adventuresome group carried a suffrage banner to the top of Mt. Rainier. Adella Parker, a graduate of the University of Washington Law School, founded her own newspaper, *The Western Woman Voter,* to educate prospective voters and to advance the cause. A neophyte in the campaign was another University of Washington student, Jeanette Rankin, who made her first political speech to an audience of seven at a suffrage rally in Ballard. On return to her native Montana, Rankin was the first woman to be elected to Congress.

DeVoe's initial strategy was a quiet but powerful "still-hunt." She advocated few suffrage meetings and no parades, but plenty of speakers at supportive club, farmer, labor and church gatherings to educate the public without arousing hostility.

An equally committed but opposite personality was May Arkwright Hutton, who after venturing west with a band of prospectors and working as their cook, had struck it rich in the Coeur d'Alene mines. Before moving to Spokane in 1907, she had already voted for more than a decade in Idaho and was determined that she and other women would have the same right in Washington. Active nationally in the Democratic party and in the suffrage campaign, she counted national and local leaders along with people from her blue collar background among her friends.

Unlike the conservative DeVoe, Hutton maintained that "there's no such thing as bad publicity." Historian Lucille Fargo describes her as a "big homely, fire-eating she-dragon luxuriating in vainglorious clothes and expounding her particular brand of horse sense in the adulterated language of the horse trader."[4] In her scarlet auto, May Hutton and other suffragists drove around the country, singing campaign songs and giving speeches wherever a crowd assembled. She attracted considerable attention in a Spokane parade, when "she rode through the streets on a float personifying 'Woman' and companioned by two denizens of the zoo, one in chains, the other obviously lacking in mental equipment. 'Criminals and idiots can't vote, and neither can women,' was the gist of the legend emblazoned on the float."[5]

To DeVoe's and like-minded ladies' chagrin, Hutton descended on Olympia as chaperone for "eight fair daughters" from Spokane, who "in their finest gowns and jewels" lobbied legislators at the Inaugural Ball. When the legislature voted overwhelmingly to submit the suffrage measure

Women's suffrage was a popular topic for political cartoonists. (Courtesy of Ross K. Rieder)

May Hutton (seated left with her husband Al standing behind her) and her women friends had voted for 10 years in Idaho, before the Huttons moved to Spokane. Here, they ride on a railroad handcar to a picnic spot near Kellogg. (Courtesy of the Eastern Washington State Historical Society, #768)

to the voters, DeVoe breathed a sigh of relief, saying that Hutton had nearly ruined their cause; Hutton on the other hand claimed credit for the victory. The result was that the dominant DeVoe faction ousted Hutton from the association. In Spokane, her supporters formed their own Political Equality League proclaiming May Hutton as president.

In 1909, the National American Suffrage Association held its convention in Seattle during the Alaska-Yukon-Pacific Exposition. Hutton and a sizable eastern Washington contingent met the "suffrage train" and entertained national leaders in Spokane before joining them for the last leg of their journey. At the convention, the bickering about strategy between the DeVoe and Hutton factions peaked, resulting in two Washington delegations, each of which demanded to be seated. In what the press called a "Solomon's judgment," the NASA seated both groups, but neither was allowed to vote.

In spite of the fracas, the campaign moved ahead. On November 8, 1910, Washington voters passed the suffrage referendum by a majority of almost two to one. Breaking a 15-year period of doldrums, Washington thus became the fifth state in the nation to enfranchise women.

Municipal Housekeeping

As in 1886, the women's vote meant social reform, but this time there was no thought of its being imperiled. Progressivism had infused all parts of the nation with different factions trying to clean up big business, government, the political system and society as a whole. In Washington State the women's vote tipped the balance of power in favor of the reformers with an ensuing clampdown on corruption.

One of the most dramatic cleanup operations took place in Seattle, where saloons and brothels operated openly. The city's Federation of Women's Clubs, the WCTU, the Women's Suffrage Association and the Mothers' Congress acted quickly to exercise their voters' rights by organizing a recall campaign against Mayor Hiram Gill. "Gill had broken his pre-election promise to confine sin to the Skid Road area, and had instead granted sanction to his cronies to build the world's largest brothel—250 rooms—on a city street. With the campaign slogan, 'Ladies: Get Out and Hustle!,' Seattle's newly enfranchised voters ensured Gill's defeat in 1911, and the intended brothel, which never opened, was converted into a legitimate rooming house."[6]

Similarly, Emma DeVoe led outraged Tacoma women to recall Mayor Angelo Fawcett. Historian Murray Morgan says, "Earlier Fawcett had been asked by businessmen to do something about a house of prostitution on Pacific Avenue. He arranged a trade for city property on A Street—off the main drag. To businessmen this was OK, but for the women it was an endorsement of Sodom, Gomorrah, and the Seattle Skid Road."[7]

At the helm of social progressivism, women made headway in other directions. They won public kindergartens and support for rural schools; they rejoiced when the legislature enacted a $10.00 per week minimum wage for working women; and they successfully advocated for jail matrons to deal with female prisoners and for juvenile courts.

The zeal for moral reform was pandemic, resulting in Washington's passage of dry laws in 1914, followed five years later by the Volstead Act that prohibited manufacture or sale of liquor throughout the nation, except for druggists. Running on reform tickets, both Gill and Fawcett were re-elected as mayors of their respective cities in 1914. To the consternation of their former pals, both called out the vice squads with strict instructions to enforce the law and to keep their cities pure and "dry."

As president of the Seattle's YWCA and WCTU, Emma Wallingford Wood proposed even more ambitious tactics for preventing young people from going astray. She said, "There are dance halls, parks and playfields which should be visited, not to speak of the young couples met on the streets,

Members of the Seattle Federation of Women's Clubs and the Mothers' Congress
issued "An Appeal to Mothers and Fathers" in their campaign to recall Mayor
Hiram Gill. (Courtesy of Special Collections Div., Univ. of Washington Libraries,
UW Neg. #8283.)

The "world's largest brothel" was situated on an unfinished Seattle street.
(Courtesy of Special Collections Div., Univ. of Washington Libraries, UW Neg.
#8235)

With their banner aloft and their children in tow, members of this Spokane
WCTU chapter meet in 1916. (Courtesy of the Eastern Washington State
Historical Society, Spokane)

many of whom, if followed and watched, might be spared a life of regret."[8]
Throughout the state, neighborhood theaters replaced saloons; automobile
and home ownership were on the upswing; the war in Europe fueled employment and prosperity; and the bourgeois emphasis was on families and
clean living. Bootleggers had begun operations.

Notes

1. See Karen J. Blair, *The Clubwoman as Feminist: True Womanhood Redefined,
   1868–1914* (New York, 1980). Blair discusses founding and development of
   eastern women's clubs in a movement that she calls "Domestic Feminism."
2. *Washington Standard* (Olympia, Aug. 19, 1871).
3. Lucy B. Thomas, Descriptions of women's activities in early Yakima, W.P.A.
   Federal Writers' Project: Women in State Development, 1930s, Washington
   State Historical Society.
4. T. A. Larson, "The Woman Suffrage Movement in Washington," *Pacific
   Northwest Quarterly* (April, 1976), p. 56.
5. Lucille Fargo, *Spokane Story* (Minneapolis: Northwestern Press, 1957), p. 240.
6. Mildred Andrews, *Seattle Women: a Legacy of Community Development* (Seattle: YWCA, 1984), p. 15.
7. Murray Morgan, *Puget's Sound: Narrative of Early Tacoma and South Sound*
   (Seattle and London: University of Washington Press, 1979), p. 323.
8. Emma Wood. Quoted from Austin E. Griffith's Papers, File 7–19, 1913, University of Washington Manuscripts Collection.

Club women met in the Seattle YWCA's tea room, where they often formulated tactics to promote social reform. 1914.
(YWCA of Seattle/King County Records, University of Washington Libraries)

Politics and Advocacy

2

While women in most of the southern and eastern states were still embrangled in their suffrage campaigns, western women began to venture into the male dominion of politics. May Hutton again made headlines in 1912, when she took Baltimore by storm as the first woman delegate to a national Democratic convention. In the same year, King County's Nina Jolidon Croake and Whatcom County's Frances Axtell were the first women to win elections to the State House of Representatives. Although both had advanced college degrees and were well informed, they were regarded primarily as novelties in a formerly all-male club, and neither served a second term. Walla Walla's Josephine Corliss Preston (discussed in the chapter on education) was elected State Superintendent of Schools in 1912, and in 1914, Seattle's Rhea Whitehead broke into the judicial hierarchy as Washington's first female Justice of the Peace.

Political Pioneers

In 1922, Spokane voters elected attorney, Reba Hurn, as the state's pioneer woman senator. A staunch Prohibitionist, Hurn had the backing of women's groups and of men who deplored political corruption, especially if it condoned "wetness." Perhaps her greatest hurdle was the sleezy image of political backrooms, themselves, which the proper public saw as no place for a lady. Her perfunctory response was: "Pooh! . . . Women have been granted equal rights by the majority of the male voters, and there is no reason women should further ignore public service. . . . I am qualified for the right to run for it, and am in the race."[1]

When Hurn arrived in Olympia, the Senate honored her by allocating funds for a women's lounge—unthought of when the old capitol was built. In a gesture rarely made to freshman senators, her peers made her chairman of the State Libraries and Public Morals Committees (both of which were outgrowths of earlier club women's advocacy, and both of which neatly fit into women's traditional roles). Historian Kathryn Hinsch says: "Reba worked diligently to be accepted as an equal member of the body but it was difficult as the only woman. At the end of her first session, the senators awarded Reba a diamond pin for 'acting like a lady.' Unfortunately, 'acting like a lady' meant saying little, being content to keep to women's concerns, and most importantly, not questioning the behavior of her colleagues. Reba was careful to stay within her boundaries. She had done a great service for women by being elected to the Senate. She saw no reason to rock the boat."[2]

Another woman, elected to the House of Representatives in 1922, was Wenatchee's Belle Culp Reeves. A former newspaperwoman and teacher,

A former teacher, Carrie Shumway was elected to the Kirkland City Council in 1911—the first woman in the state to hold the position. (Courtesy of the Seattle Public Schools Archives)

Seattle Mayor Bertha Knight Landes breaks ground for the new Civic Auditorium in 1926. It was remodelled in preparation for the 1961 Worlds Fair to become the city's opera house. (Courtesy of Special Collections Div., Univ. of Washington Libraries, UW Neg. #343)

18

she had devoted her energies to civic, cultural and educational activities in her community. Thanks to her women friends, who just a few days before the primary had persuaded her to run, she won the election as a write-in candidate. Although her husband, a former legislator and a judge, was less than enthusiastic about her victory, he gave her his full support.

Belle Reeves entered the House as one of four Democrats and was frequently the only woman legislator. By working diligently and effectively to promote various social causes, she succeeded in winning the admiration of her male peers. In 1938, she was appointed Secretary of State (the first and only woman to hold the office) and occasionally served as acting governor. In her acceptance speech, she said: "My real job, and the biggest way I can help women of this state, in my office, is to conduct myself so as to be a credit to my sex."[3] One of her lasting legacies was her support of other qualified women, whom she sought out and encouraged to seek office.

There were also political pioneers at the community level. Of particular interest is Seattle's Bertha Knight Landes, a devoted homemaker whose outside activities included her church, the PTA, the Washington State Soroptimists and the Seattle Federation of Women's Clubs. With her club sisters managing her campaign for City Council, Landes won by a landslide. As acting mayor, she attracted national attention when she fired the chief of police, a man who boasted publicly about corruption in his department. She immediately cracked down on free-wheeling bootleggers and saw that regulations for dance halls and cabarets were enforced.

In 1926, running on a platform that stressed law enforcement, reform and morality, she defeated incumbant, Edwin J. "Doc" Brown, to become the first woman mayor of any major American city. Although her administration received high marks, she lost the next election to a political unknown. Among other things, she attributed her defeat to her opponent's lavish campaign budget and to "sex prejudice."

For the press, the issue of her sex had consistently superseded her accomplishments in office with an overriding sentiment that a city of stature should have a man at the helm. Near the end of her term, she summed up her political philosophy: "Municipal housekeeping means adventure and romance and accomplishment to me. To be in some degree a guiding force in the destiny of a city, to help lay the foundation stones for making it good and great, to aid in advancing the political position of women . . . to spread the political philosophy that the city is only a larger home—I find it richly worthwhile."[4]

In 1916, Anna Louise Strong, a former officer in the Child Welfare Society, was the first woman to be elected to the Seattle School Board. Two years later, she was recalled by a narrow margin because of her opposition to the war and the draft. Women's organizations, labor, and churches were on record as staunch advocates for peace, but patriotism and the "War to End All Wars" had taken precedence. In the post-war period, local women founded chapters of the newly formed Women's International League for Peace and Freedom. (Courtesy of Special Collections Div., Univ. of Washington Libraries, UW Neg. #340)

Political Organizations

Washington women continued to campaign for national suffrage until 1920, when voters ratified the 19th Amendment to the United States Constitution. Historians have frequently argued that the women's movement came to a virtual halt at this point. Their reasoning is as follows. During World War I, women kept the home fires burning, filling in for men in the work force, while making enormous contributions through relief work. Following the Armistice, men throughout the country were in a mood to reward women by granting them suffrage. With the right to vote, peace, and postwar efforts to return to normal, married women (who had entered the labor force during the wartime emergency) went home, content with wifedom, motherhood and gardening. Most women were under the illusion that the vote would give them full equality with men. However, they failed to take into account existing patterns of power, where men dominated as heads of state, church, the family and business. Historians who promote this point of view often cite the National Women's Party, founded by Alice Paul as a singular exception. Paul's proposed Equal Rights Amendment to the United States Constitution became the sole issue of her party, whose membership included only the most stalwart feminists.

In actuality, the amount of organized political activity on the part of women did decrease dramatically in the 1920s. However, to say that it came to an abrupt halt is hyperbole. While women would never again have the unity of purpose and the crusading strength of the suffragists, many nonetheless took seriously their new rights and responsibilities as voters by participating actively in established political parties and in political organizations of their own. Nowhere is this more evident than in Washington State, where women had already voted for 10 years and where a strong farmer-labor alliance, coupled with Populism and Progressivism, had bred a liberal climate, conducive to social reform.

League of Women Voters

Just before the passage of the Equal Suffrage Amendment in 1920, Carrie Chapman Catt issued a call to organize the non-partisan National League of Women Voters. Its purpose was to educate women for citizenship, so that they could work within the parties of their choice. The LWV had antecedents in the non-partisan National Council of Women Voters, founded in 1910 by Emma Smith DeVoe. At DeVoe's invitation, the governors of each of the five equal suffrage states had appointed women commissioners to attend an inaugural meeting, held at the home of Virginia Wilson Mason in Tacoma. The objects of the council were "to obtain equal suffrage in other states; to change conditions in our own states for the betterment of men and women, of children and the home, and to claim justice for women in the political, social and economic world."[5] By 1920, the organization was well established and had affiliated with the National American Women's Suffrage Association.

However, for years an antagonism had raged between eastern and western suffragists. During their earlier crusade, Abigail Scott Duniway, Emma DeVoe, and other northwest suffragists had done their best to keep eastern leaders from intruding and upsetting their "still-hunt" strategy. Later, victorious northwesterners, who continued to campaign for national suffrage, gave freely of their own unsolicited advice. DeVoe admonished "the non-voting suffragists of the East [to] cease publishing their bickerings and jealousies and concentrate their energies on the vital issue, woman suffrage."[6]

As in Washington's earlier crusade, there were tactical schisms in the national movement. Most western women voters sided with Alice Paul's Congressional Union, which the NAWSA repudiated for refusing to follow directions. Due to the East-West antagonism, Catt, as president of the NAWSA, virtually nullified the organizational achievements of northwestern women by supplanting their National Council of Women Voters with her own National League of Women Voters.

Because of the affront and lingering hurt, the LWV was slow to take root in Washington's communities, but in time the wounds began to heal. Through the years, the LWV has emphasized study and discussion, acting on issues only on consensus of opinion. Due to its unbiased and thorough process, it has earned a reputation for sound judgment and has frequently influenced the action of both male and female voters. In its early history, some were critical of the league for its policy of not endorsing candidates, especially women who were running for office. Others, however, credited their LWV experience with teaching them the necessary organizational and leadership skills to work effectively within the political system.

Women's Legislative Council of Washington

As an alternative to the LWV, many politically-minded women joined the non-partisan Women's Legislative Council of Washington. Organized in 1917, it owed its beginnings to Seattle's North End Progressive Club, which had issued a call to women's clubs throughout the state to join. With a membership that peaked at 140 clubs and that also included individuals, the organization's purpose was to investigate and initiate measures to bring before the lawmaking bodies. It also sought to educate women about their legal rights and responsibilities and to foster in them an interest in politics. Its motto, "Arise ye women that are at ease,!" meant that the welfare of other women was the concern of every woman. Like the National Women's Party, the organization lobbied during the 1920s and 1930s for legislation to give women equal rights with men.

Members of local councils met bi-monthly and twice a year they sent delegates to conventions, hosted in different cities throughout the state. Sophie L. W. Clark, editor of the WLCW's newsletter, the *Legislative Counsellor*, endeavored to report in an unbiased manner, even on issues where the members were in strong agreement. Learned contributors to the *Counsellor* included Tacoma's Dr. Alice Maude Smith, who wrote about health care issues, and Seattle lawyer Lady Willie Forbus, who helped to educate women regarding the legislative process.

Among the issues that the WLCW addressed were child labor laws, education and vocational training, and existing laws that discriminated against women. Between 1919 and 1927, the organization's intense lobbying efforts helped to secure passage of 59 measures. Examples were equal pay for male and female teachers and equal representation for women on precinct committees.

Although its membership was largely white and middle-class, the WLCW concerned itself with issues that affected people of color. It supported a bill to construct permanent buildings for the Tulalip Indian High School. It also urged members to contribute to the Sojourner Truth Home, founded in Seattle by the State Federation of Colored Women's Clubs to care for single black women. On the national level, it joined forces with the state's black organizations to lobby for passage of an anti-lynching bill.

Black Women's Alliances

Under the leadership of Alice Presto and Alley Duppee, black women in Washington formed their own Women's Political and Civic Alliance, modeled on lines similar to the WLCW. The organization encouraged black people to use the ballot and work for the welfare of their race. Politics were nothing new to the state's black women. In 1912, when the National Association for the Advancement of Colored People was just three years old, Tacoma's Nettie Asberry had established a local branch—the first one west of the Rockies—and had gone on to organize chapters in Spokane, Seattle and Portland. During the 1920s, black women's organizations and the NAACP helped to garner public support for effectively limiting the power of the Ku Klux Klan, which in the early 1920s had more than 40,000 members (some of whom were women) in the state. In Tacoma, the NAACP led an interracial rally to prevent the showing of "Birth of a Nation," which portrayed the Klan as heroic.

Music teacher, Nettie Asberry of Tacoma, founded chapters of the NAACP in her own city and in Seattle, Spokane, and Portland. The national organization praised her for her accomplishments. She was also a prime mover in Washington's State Federation of Colored Women's Clubs. (Nettie Asberry Papers, University of Washington Libraries)

In Spokane, a drug store owner refused to serve two black patrons. The two, who had previously received courteous service at the store, became the object of a civil case which Judge Girard planned to present in Olympia. When the Klan left an intimidating warning note on the door of the Bethel Church, it aroused the ire of the black community and many others. Historian Joe Franklin cites the following quotes that appeared in the *Spokesman Review:* "Mrs. A. C. Houston, Vice President of the State Federation of Negro Women Clubs, . . . demanded that blacks in the Northwest be treated as citizens. Mrs. Bertha Carvens, who was President of the City Federation declared 'this is not an individual case, the outcome of this case will affect every Negro in the Community.' Another woman said, 'I live near the drug store in question and until this incident, Negro people had always been treated well.' "[7]

The Spokane Police Department put a ban on parades and meetings of masked people. Franklin's summation of the Klan's activity in Spokane

Black women at a gathering in Spokane in 1923, where six years earlier, the State Association of Colored Women's Clubs was organized. The association gave financial backing to the Sojourner Truth Clubhouse, established in Seattle to provide affordable housing for black women. (Courtesy of the Eastern Washington State Historical Society, Spokane, #L86–588,360)

is typical of events elsewhere in Washington: "Spokane's small black community represented no real threat to the livelihood of the dominant population or to the Ku Klux Klan itself. Additionally the strong stands taken by the People of Spokane, the newspapers, the police department, and the black community set effective limits to Klan activities."[8]

Labor Union Women

Another women's political alliance was the Federation of Union Women and Auxiliaries, which formed in Seattle in 1916. It was composed of trade union women, women's auxiliaries affiliated with trade unions and Union Card and Label League. Up to that time, women's unions had operated independently within the Washington State Federation of Labor and their local Central Labor Councils, lending their support to the bodies as a whole. However, as their numbers increased and as their special concerns became more evident, Seattle women workers decided that they needed an additional federation of their own.

A key organizer was Alice Lord, who in 1900 had sparked the formation of the Seattle Waitresses' Union, one of the first women's unions to be chartered by the American Federation of Labor. Lord had no illusions about the need for further protections for working women and like other working-class suffragists, she had a triple agenda: to win the franchise, to improve the status of working women, and to promote the rights and opportunities of the working class as a whole. Waitresses' Local 240 began by learning the tactics of strikes, negotiations, organizing, and lobbying.

There were several factors that thrust increasing numbers of early 20th century women into the work force, among them urbanization, industrialization, periodic recessions, immigration and World War I. Turn-of-the-century waitresses often worked 14-hour days, seven days a week for wages of $3.00 to $6.00 per week. Within a few years of their organization, Seattle waitresses had a union contract limiting their schedule to 10 hours a day, six days a week, with a minimum salary of $8.50.[9]

Their early dedication to union issues had earned the waitresses backing from the male-dominated Washington State Federation of Labor, so that they were able to launch a statewide campaign to improve conditions for

Alice Seaton, delivering the mail—a nontraditional job. According to her sister, Esther Rorrison, Seaton was the first woman mail carrier in the United States. When her husband became ill in 1915, she took over his Rural Route 1 in Bothell. In addition to her job, she cared for her husband, four children and two horses. (Washington Women's Heritage Project Records, University of Washington Libraries)

When the local chapter of Journeymen Barbers International refused membership to women, the Seattle Central Labor Council granted them their own charter for a Lady Barbers Union. 1904 photo. (Courtesy of Special Collections Div., Univ. of Washington Archives, Neg. #8694)

working women. Alice Lord led a coalition of the Washington State Federation of Women's Clubs, the Ministerial Alliance, organized labor, and others to Olympia to lobby for the eight-hour day. One of their arguments, which closely resembled the club woman's ethic, was that the shorter workday would give a woman the chance to educate herself and to elevate her position in society.

The "Waitresses' Bill," originally proposed in 1904, gained passage in 1911, when the Washington State Legislature became one of the first in the nation to enact the eight-hour day for women, (excluding cannery, fruit and domestic workers). Two years later, a minimum-wage bill for women workers won wide-spread support, partially because of reformers who blamed low wages for forcing women into prostitution.

Recognizing strength in numbers, the waitresses helped other groups of union women to organize, among them garment workers, hotel and do-mestic maids, and the Seattle Union Card and Label League. The latter was an influential auxiliary, composed of wives and female relatives of union men, whose major objective was to support the unions. The leagues promoted the use of union-made products to consumers, fed union families during strikes, assisted unemployed union women, and helped organize boycotts of businesses that rejected union demands. As other Card and Label Leagues took root in Spokane, Yakima, Walla Walla, Everett, Aberdeen, Olympia, and Tacoma, they became an effective statewide lobbying force.

The leagues forged a bridge between the federation of working women and middle-class club women who together, as members of the Women's Legislative Council of Washington, lobbied for day nurseries for children of working mothers, abolition of child labor, and equal pay for equal work. The local coalition supported the National Women's Trade Union League in its campaign for the eight-hour day and a consequent death knell to sweatshops, still commonplace in the East.

World War I brought unprecedented numbers of women into the work force. At the time, many classifications of women workers remained unorganized and consequently powerless to improve their conditions of employment. In Seattle, the federated union women persuaded the Central Labor Council to hire a woman organizer. Blanche Johnson was the catalyst for several new unions, including women telephone operators, shoemakers, barbers and elevator operators. In 1818, when "hello girls" went on strike for higher pay, the Brotherhood of Electrical Workers joined them, crippling phone service up and down the coast until employers agreed to negotiate.

During World War I, as later in World War II, women proved that they could handle jobs previously considered "men's work." Employers, who raved about women workers' efficiency, often fattened their coffers since they could pay a woman less than a man for the same job. While women trumpeted the campaign for equal pay for equal work, they were vulnerable in non-traditional jobs, where male-dominated unions only rarely gave them strong backing. Exceptions included Seattle machinists and electricians who during the crisis recruited women workers on the same basis as men. Following the Armistice and the return of male veterans, working women quickly moved back into traditionally female jobs with traditionally dimunitive paychecks.

In late 1919, Seattle union women supported the city's shipyard workers in what became the nation's first general strike. For five days, the highly unionized city was virtually shut down with only emergency services and soup kitchens in operation. When the non-violent strike ended, labor had

Seattle's candy workers had their own union./These members ply their trade at the candy counter of the downtown Bon Marche. (Courtesy of the Washington State Historical Society, Tacoma, Photo #26268)

Wives of AFL trade union members joined the Union Card and Label League to promote union-made products. Here they staff their exhibit at the Spokane Interstate Fair (1914). (Courtesy of the Eastern Washington State Historical Society, Spokane, #L83–181.7)

Women laundry workers were early unionizers in Washington's larger communities. However, women, such as these, who set up shop near mining and logging camps were generally isolated from the trade unions. Ferry County, ca. 1899. (Courtesy of the Eastern Washington State Historical Society, Spokane, #L84–423.115.2)

International Brotherhood of Electrical Workers Local 77 of Seattle joins "Hello Girls" on strike in 1918, with other strikes following in Tacoma and Aberdeen and on the Oregon and California coasts. When war production was threatened, President Wilson stepped in to negotiate a settlement. (Courtesy of the Pacific Northwest Labor History Association)

World War I crew of section hands on the Northern Pacific tracks. (Courtesy of the Skagit County Historical Society)

Elizabeth Gurley Flynn—later popularized in a Joe Hill tune as "The Rebel Girl"—used biting wit to lambaste authority and fire up crowds of tatterdemalions and itinerant workers, who converged on Spokane in 1919. The Industrial Workers of the World "Wobblies," founded in Chicago in 1905, wanted to organize all workers into One Big Union that would rule society and end the reign of greedy capitalists. Hundreds were arrested in Spokane for illegal assembly on city streets. (Courtesy of Special Collections Div., Univ. of Washington, Neg. #341)

While the Wobblies purported to speak for all workers, their main constituency was the unskilled laborer, including women, immigrants and ethnic minorities. One of their strongholds was the Pacific Northwest with its dependence on migratory farm hands and lumberjacks. These hops harvesters in Whatcom County—men, women and families of different ethnic groups—could have been members. (Courtesy of Special Collections Div., Univ. of Washington, Neg. #2032)

Miners' wives stood on the picket line during strikes. When boxes of clothing and food arrived from the union, the women distributed them to needy families. Recalcitrant mine owners recruited immigrants (many of them from eastern and southern Europe) and black miners from other states. When hostilities quieted down, many of the newcomers stayed. Roslyn developed in this manner, becoming one of the most ethnically diverse communities in the state. Ethel Florence Craven, shown here with her mother Harriet Jackson Taylor, still makes Roslyn her home and remains a link to the initial migration of black people. (Courtesy of the Ellensburg Public Library)

Cheng Hiang with her husband, the Rev. Joseck S. Hwang, and their daughters immigrated from China to Seattle in 1909, when there were only a few Chinese families in the state. When the Baptist minister moved on to New York, his wife, who did not speak English, had to support the family herself. With the help of her daughters, she opened the Chinese Embroidery Shop in downtown Seattle. She occasionally moved her shop from Seattle to Yakima and to Spokane, and for 52 years, she sold embroidery from her booth at the Puyallup Fair. Eventually, all six daughters went to the university, becoming respectively an M.D., a librarian, a dietician, a pharmicist, a teacher and an artist. 1921 photo. (Courtesy of Priscilla Chong Jue)

proved that it could temporarily cripple the city, but little else. Exacerbating a turn of public sentiment were the Bolshevik Revolution in Russia and vituperative demonstrations by the radical Industrial Workers of the World (Wobblies) who had migrated to lumber camps and wheat fields throughout the state. A cautious middle class began to link labor's demands with a call for revolution. The result was an "open shop" movement among many employers who had previously supported the unions. When the Union Card and Label League later attempted to organize a consumer boycott against the Bon Marche for what the union considered to be unfair practices, clubwomen no longer supported their cause.

Business and Professional Women

Among women workers who had not unionized were business "girls," as they called themselves. Seattle's Business Girls' Club began in 1913 at the YWCA, followed by other clubs throughout the state. Members viewed their affiliation, along with the typewriter, as their entrance to the business world. In 1921, just two years after the national federation was formed, Seattle's Bess Snow McCallum extended a call to clubs throughout the state to "mobilize, organize and vitalize" by founding the Washington State Federation of Business and Professional Women's Clubs. The throng of 400 women, representing ten different clubs from nine cities, elected Seattle's Lulu M. Fairbanks as president. While members regarded their initial convention as an unqualified success, their second meeting in Wenatchee exceeded all expectations, attracting 1,273 participants from 22 different clubs and making the Washington federation the second largest in the nation.

Along with an emphasis on community service, the clubs emphasized self-improvement of members. Evangeline Starr, who succeeds Rhea Whitehead as Justice of the Peace, recalls the early Seattle First BPW: "In the early days our club had programs, not only for education and making us better in the office, but also for making us as individuals more competent too." Judge Starr was twice elected State President and worked on both State and National BPW Legislative Committees to promote the status of women.

The Women's Movement: Now and Then

While a few exceptional women made inroads into the male bastions of power, and while women's political organizations could claim occasional victories (primarily in social reform and good government reform activities), most of women's collective work centered on betterment of the community, betterment of others, and betterment of themselves. Judge Starr has been a life-long activist nationally and locally in women's clubs, political organizations and professional societies. When asked for a general characterization of women's mission after 1920, she said: "One of the things I've thought of with all of this women's work is their humility, their complete humility . . . wanting to make things better. There was never any feeling of command or demand until the era of NOW (the National Organization for Women). It started in Washington, D.C. [A friend] wrote me a letter [to ask if] I would like to belong, and I sent in my $5.00. . . . That's when women started to demand, but before that they had been very

The typewriter opened the door for women to the business world. Seattle First National Bank, 1905. (Courtesy of Special Collections Div., Univ. of Washington Libraries, UW Neg. #2084)

Convention of Washington State Business and Professional Women's Club in Wenatchee, 1922. (Courtesy of the Everett Public Library)

The Boeing Company hired women during World War I to fabricate airplane wings. (Courtesy of The Boeing Company Archives)

These "Rosies" kept The Boeing Company going during World War II. For the first time, the company hired minority women. (Courtesy of The Boeing Company Archives)

humble . . . we just wanted to be better, to make things better, but then we began to say 'We deserve something,' too."

The first local chapter of NOW was formed in Judge Starr's chambers in 1970. Other organizations soon followed, including the Washington Women's Political Caucus, Washington Women United, Elected Wash-

ington Women, and others, while many established federations lent their support. Between the 1930s and 1970s, there were some gains in social reform, especially in the areas of child care and civil rights. However, the most significant breakthroughs for women's issues have usually occurred during periods of a strong women's movement. In the 1880s, the early 19th century, the teens, and the 1970s and 1980s, Washington women rallied to demand changes in the law.

The contemporary women's movement gave rise to unprecedented opportunities for women in non-traditional fields, ranging from blue-collar trades to leadership positions in business and in politics. In 1972, voters elected Dixy Lee Ray to serve as Washington State's first woman governor. In 1982, women comprised 23% of the state legislature, where they served in leadership positions on a broad spectrum of committees. The ranks of women judges also swelled as women broke the barriers to appointments in the higher courts. As women broadened their power base, they were able to bring women's issues into the mainstream of political concern.

Like the early suffragists, modern proponents of the Equal Rights Amendment and Comparable Worth have waged strenuous campaigns to overcome injustices that they perceived. A traditionally liberal state, Washington has frequently been a national pacesetter where women's issues are concerned. Its passage of women's suffrage, prohibition, comparable worth legislation, the Equal Rights Amendment, and more have paved the way for similar legislation nationally and in other states.

Notes

1. Kathryn Hinsch, ed., *Political Pioneers: a Study of Women in the Washington State Legislature* (Elected Washington Women, 1983), p. 3.
2. Ibid. p. 4.
3. Ibid. p. 54.
4. Doris Pieroth, "Seattle's Woman Mayor," in James Warren, *King County and Its Queen City* (Seattle, 1981), p. 129.
5. Abigail Scott Duniway, *Path Breaking: an Autobiographical History of the Equal Suffrage Movement in Pacific Coast States* (New York, 1971— reprinted from James, Kerns & Abbott edition of 1914), p. 246.
6. Ruth Barnes Moynihan, *Rebel for Rights* (New Haven and London: 1983), p. 217.
7. Joe Franklin, "The Ku Klux Klan in the City of Spokane, 1921–1924," *Pacific Northwest Forum,* Vol. XI, #1, Winter, 1986, p. 20.
8. Ibid.
9. "News of the Waitresses' Association," *Seattle Union Record,* Feb. 8, 1902, p. 8. The daily paper was the official organ of the Washington State Federation of Labor.

Gathering herbs, roots and grain was a time-honored responsibility of Native American women who often shared their knowledge and remedies with new settlers. This Makah woman gathers grain in the traditional way. Photo by Asahel Curtis.
(Courtesy of the Washington State Historical Society, #44154)

Health Care **3**

As care givers for the sick and injured, women have a legacy that pervades almost every culture. Traditionally, Native American women have served as midwives, herbologists and "shamen" (medicine women). Black pioneers who ventured west often called on "Granny women" or "Grannies" for health care, while immigrant Chinese depended on women trained in the spiritual and healing arts.

Shamen and Midwives

To early Washington women, cultural barriers at times seemed transparent. When Seattle's first white settlers came ashore in 1851, Mary Denny was unable to produce enough milk to nourish her new-born baby. Recognizing the problem, a native Salish woman introducd her to clam nectar which is said to have saved the baby's life. In Hoquiam, early settlers turned to Shoalwater shamen, one of whom they affectionately called "Dr. Kate." Irene Shale, a modern-day Shoalwater tribal elder, recounts family stories of grateful settlers who sometimes gave gifts to her grandmother in appreciation for her "doctoring" services. According to Shale, "they said she cured someone of great standing here on the bay and they gave her a necklace of fire. And my dad said it must have been a diamond necklace. They said it looked like fire around her neck. . . ."[1]

Among white settlers, health care was also predominantly women's work. Well into the 20th century, residents of sparsely populated rural areas relied on women with a knowledge of home remedies. On San Juan Island, people sent for Lucinda Boyce who traveled on horseback to make house calls. Pioneer Mary Jane Fraser reminisced: "When father was kicked by a horse and considerably hurt, Boyce was called and used her favorite aid, a bread and milk poltice. She never lost a case in childbirth."[2] In central Washington's Douglas County, pioneer mothers relied on Charlotte Meyer Fisher, a Norwegian immigrant trained in nursing. She later recalled: "When I first came here, there was no doctor to help the poor women with their babies. I was a midwife. . . ."[3] To the south Benton County's Jane Shaw not only treated families suffering from contagious diseases; she also brought them food, clothing, and even flowers.

Pioneer Women Doctors

As trained—usually male—doctors came into communities, the women who had preceded them generally stepped back. Among Washington's most resolute pioneers were a few white women who themselves became licensed physicians. In the Victorian era, they often had to deal with prejudice not only within the medical establishment, but also in the community at large.

Women in the booming mining town of Newcastle (King County) on an outing to gather ferns. Georgianna Rouse (standing, fourth from left) was the mother of 11 children and served as mid-wife to many of her neighbors. (Courtesy of Mary J. Rouse)

In 1898, 60-year-old Dr. Bethenia Owens-Adair moved from Oregon to Yakima, anticipating a rest from her demanding practice. But in the epidemic ridden community, she was soon making house calls, driving her horse and buggy from farmhouse to farmhouse day and night. When in one home, death claimed a beautiful young girl, the mother became hysterical, while her pregnant sister-in-law went into premature labor. Owens-Adair called the public health officer to demand that he immediately remove the corpse because a baby was about to be born. The health officer said that he was enjoying an Elks celebration and that he and the undertaker would come in the morning. There is no record of their further discussion, but the doctor later reported that both men came that night.

Such struggles were nothing new to Owens-Adair who had pursued a medical career at a time when women doctors were considered an oddity. An Oregon pioneer, she had raised her son alone and at age 40 had abandoned her successful millinery business to enroll in the Eclectic School of Medicine in Philadelphia (one of the few that would accept women). By the time that she came to Yakima, she was a respected physician who had overcome sometimes hostile sentiment on the part of the public as well as the male medical establishment.

Like other early women doctors in the Northwest, Owens-Adair had a strong sense of social responsibility. A determined lobbyist for the Women's Christian Temperance Union, women's suffrage, and other social causes, she wrote editorials and gave speeches to thousands.

She also urged women to exercise regularly and frequently spoke out for less restrictive women's clothing. In a 1904 letter to *The Seattle Times*, she took Dr. Montegue Tallock to task for advocating side saddle as the proper mode of riding for ladies. She wrote: "Ladies should ride astride. . . . Nothing will preserve women's grace . . . so much as vigorous . . . exercise, and horse-back riding stands at the head of the list, provided (a woman has) a foot in each stirrup, instead of having the right limb twisted about a horn, and the left foot in a stirrup 12 or 15 inches above where it ought to be."

Unlike Dr. Owens-Adair, Spokane's Dr. Mary Archard Latham gained ready acceptance from both the medical establishment and the community. A graduate of the Cincinnati College of Medicine and Surgery, she was Washington's first "regular" woman physician and was considered by many to be one of the state's best doctors. Prior to coming to Spokane in 1888, Latham was a member of the first class of women to be admitted as students to the clinical wards of Cincinnati General Hospital.

Dr. Mary A. Latham. Photo by Maxwell. (Courtesy of the Spokane Public Library, Northwest Room)

Like many early women doctors, her specialty was women's and children's diseases. By a unanimous vote, the directors of Spokane's Bio-Chemic College elected her to the professorship of obstetrics. But the crowning glory of her career was the hospital for women, established for her in Spokane's Lidgerwood district.

Latham came to Spokane in her mid 40s with her husband—also a physician—and their three sons. When her husband later moved to the Okanogan Reservation to continue his practice among the Indians, she remained in the city. As a result of her upbringing and her early education at Claremont Academy in Ohio, she was a lady of refinement. She was also civic spirited and just what bustling, boisterous Spokane needed as it mushroomed into the Inland Empire's major city. Among her activities, she played a leadership role in establishing the Spokane Public Library; for several years she was head of the Spokane Children's Home; she was a director for the Humane Society; and she also wrote articles and literary pieces for newspapers and magazines.

By the early 20th century, there were several women doctors practicing in Washington. Like Bethenia Owens-Adair and Mary Latham, others were involved in a wide range of social causes that extended far beyond their professional obligations. Seattle's Dr. Cora Eaton was a prime mover in the state's suffrage campaign and in environmental issues. In Tacoma, Dr. Mary Perkins met informally with other women doctors, nurses and osteopaths who eventually formed the nucleus of the local Business and Professional Women's Club. As individuals and in their affiliations, Washington's early women doctors provided role models and leadership to encourage the advancement of women both professionally and in public life.

Nursing

By the turn of the century, there were several schools of nursing in Washington state. In addition to local graduates, nurses trained elsewhere were among the newcomers who in recent years had flocked to the Northwest. Yet, anyone could call herself a nurse and among practitioners were many who had no professional certification.

Washington State Nurses

Nurses in various parts of the country had begun to organize. In 1896, they formed a national association whose purpose was to set regulatory standards both for the sake of the patient and for the advancement of women in the profession. Local nurses followed suit beginning with the organization of Spokane County Graduate Nurses in 1899. Washington nurses formed a statewide associaton and also affiliated nationally in 1908.

With the campaign for equal suffrage at full tilt, other women's organizations rallied behind the nurses to help them lobby the legislature. As a result, the governor in 1909 appointed Washington State's first board of nurse examiners, thereby recognizing the title of Registered Nurse. RNs worked in hospitals, doctors' offices, schools, and social service agencies, providing varying degrees of structured health care. With the backing of doctors, Washington nurses gained better pay and working conditions, in-

Ambulance crew, Tacoma, 1910–1912. Five women and three men staff the ambulance and tent adjacent to it. (Courtesy of the Washington State Historical Society)

cluding the eight-hour work day. Because of the hazards that they faced, nurses began to look out for themselves as well as the general public. King County nurses maintained a tuberculosis cottage for their members and for other needy nurses. The professionalization of nursing resulted in improved health care and a gradual change in public attitudes toward hospitals.

Private Duty Nursing

For decades, people had commonly objected so strongly to going to hospitals that they would ask surgeons to make house calls. Historian Anne Rafter wrote that "there was a suggestion of pauperism, of not belonging anywhere, attached to this idea of going to a hospital, especially when a new life was to be ushered into the world. It was natural and fitting that a child should be born under his father's roof, as his forbears (sic) had been."[4]

Nurses pose in front of Seattle's Swedish Hospital. (Courtesy of Special Collections Div., Univ. of Washington Libraries, UW Neg. #4661)

Some early physicians brought with them portable operating tables. As Seattle's only turn-of-the-century trained surgical nurse, Jennie Ray frequently did her best to sterilize instruments in home kitchens. If they could afford it, people hired a live-in nurse who was on call 24 hours a day. In the event that a well-to-do woman had to be hospitalized, she often brought her private nurse who slept on a cot in the patient's room.

Theresa Brown Dixon studied nursing in Vancouver and worked as a private duty nurse in Seattle from 1886 until the early 1900s. Her daughter Theresa Dixon Flowers recalls: "My father had an accident and she had to go to work. . . . She did nursing and then she did midwifery. . . . Everybody had babies at home. . . . I know times when she wouldn't get home to stay for a year. She'd go from one case to another." Mrs. Dixon's daughters, Christine Mabel and Theresa, both became nurses and each worked in the profession for more than 30 years. 1881 photo. (Courtesy of Esther Hall Mumford).

Red Cross nurses as far as the eye can see. Liberty bond parade through downtown Seattle during World War I. (Courtesy: Sisters of Providence Archives, Seattle, Washington)

Red Cross Nurses

Despite a lessening of public skepticism toward hospitals, the demand for private duty nurses remained high until the outbreak of World War I. In the name of patriotism, Red Cross recruiters trumpeted the slogan: "Luxury Nurses Must be Given Up!" When the United States entered the war in 1917, there were only 400 active duty nurses in the Army and 160 in the Navy. When the war ended in 1918, an estimated 24,000 nurses had served, caring for troops, veterans and their families both at home and abroad.

To ameliorate the sudden transition, the Red Cross offered courses in home nursing. In 1918, prior to the armistice abroad, the virulent influenza epidemic swept the nation, claiming half a million lives. Locally, graduate nurses and Red Cross volunteers ministered to flu patients in private homes and in hospitals, frequently contracting the disease themselves. In Spokane, three RNs paid for their dedication with their lives.

Public Health Nursing

The Public Health Nursing Association which had pioneered in Boston in the 1890s and gradually spread westward reached Tacoma in the early 1920s. Despite the success of Red Cross nursing programs, there was still the feeling that such efforts had been a wartime emergency measure. With life returning to normal, the medical establishment at first opposed public health plans, since they dealt with teaching and prevention measures, rather than cures and treatment. Possibly because they feared a requickening of the old anti-hospital sentiment, most doctors advocated hospitalizing sick people as patients, rather than visiting them in their homes.

Their stance however began to soften with the realization that not everyone could afford to pay a hospital bill and that barring economics, hospitals simply did not have space for everyone who needed care. Another factor was that public health nurses were certified by a different source than hospital nurses and their respective missions were not conflictive. Gradually a synergistic working relationship began to develop.

Public health nurses worked in clinics, private homes and public schools, providing care and emphasizing health education. Their mission was to give service where care was needed, regardless of creed, color or patient's ability to pay. Grace Coffman who headed the Tacoma organization in 1929 said, "While only skillful nurses are employed, if one should make a visit without leaving a thought that would germinate like a seed and bear fruit, we should count the time lost."[5] In addition to bedside care, the agency offered instruction in hygiene for different age groups, including infants, school children and pregnant mothers. It also stressed tuberculosis control and public education to control communicable diseases.

With the help of volunteers from the newly established Junior League of Tacoma, public health nurses conducted two "Well-Baby Clinics" a week at the Pierce County Hospital for Child Welfare. Mothers from all over the county brought their babies for examinations and received advice and assistance as needed. The clinics taught nutrition and hygiene with the conviction that healthy babies would require less and less medical attention as they grew older.

In communities throughout Washington, women in public health fields continued to organize under the aegises of the Red Cross, Visiting Nurses Association, Public Health Nursing Association and others. Through the years, home health care and health education instruction have taken their place within the state's medical, social service and education establishments.

Mary Abastilla Beltram (left), prior to her departure from the Philippines to America. She said, "I was in the (Philippine) Red Cross, I wanted to come and finish my B.A. in nursing. . . . The Red Cross let me come on condition I . . . remain two years . . . I didn't go back . . . I am still here." She studied at Firland Sanitarium in King County, married and worked for years as a public health nurse. (Courtesy of Demonstration Project for Asian Americans. Published in: Fred Cordova. *Filipinos: Forgotten Asian Americans*, Dubuque, 1983)

First graduating class. Fannie C. Paddock Memorial Hospital School of Nursing, Tacoma, 1897. (Courtesy of Washington State Historical Society)

Hospitals

That early Washingtonians commonly regarded health care as women's work is evident in the history of the state's hospitals. Episcopalian, Methodist and other Protestant churches elected lay women to serve as deaconesses. With the backing of their congregations, they volunteered in orphanages, hospitals, schools and in their respective parishes. In 1892, Spokane Methodists decided to name their hospital the Deaconess in recognition of the leadership of Emma Tenyard and May Raymond. Similarly, three women whose names are unrecorded opened the Spokane Protestant Sanitarium (later renamed St. Luke's Hospital) in a building owned by the Episcopal Church.

Fannie C. Paddock Memorial Hospital (now Tacoma General Hospital) was named in honor of the bishop's wife who as its benefactor began

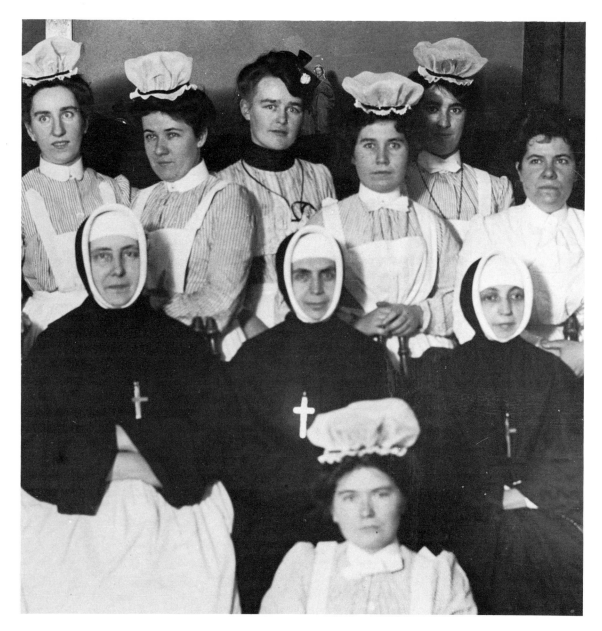

Sacred Heart Hospital, School of Nursing, Spokane. (Courtesy: Sisters of Providence Archives, Seattle, Washington)

a fundraising drive in New York City and continued it throughout the family's five-month westward migration. Protestant Episcopal Bishop John Paddock dedicated Tacoma's first hospital in 1892. His wife whose heart had gone out to the epidemic-ridden community was a victim of the journey. She died in Oregon, sending her legacy to a city that she would never see.

The Sisters of Providence

Among the first to envision organized health care in Washington was Roman Catholic Father A. M. A. Blanchet who turned to the Sisters of Providence in Montreal for help. In 1856, Mother Joseph and four other nuns set forth, arriving at Fort Vancouver on a cold December day to move into an unfinished, windowless attic. Father Blanchet was in Europe and his orders to build a convent and school had been countermanded. Undaunted, the sisters went to work. Within days they converted their space into a combination dormitory, refectory, community room and classroom. They then turned an abandoned barn into a chapel and by March had built a school and six small cabins to house orphans and boarding school pupils.

On presenting his 20-year-old daughter at the convent in Montreal, Joseph Pariseau had said, "I bring you my daughter Esther, who wishes to dedicate herself to the religious life. She can cook and sew and spin and do all manner of housework. She has learned carpentry from me . . . she will someday make a very good superior."[6] His words were prophetic.

During their first winter in Vancouver, Mother Joseph wrote to the motherhouse saying, "Beginnings are always trying, and here the devil is so enraged, he frightens me."[7] Beyond the primitive conditions and miserable coastal weather, she was concerned about how the French-speaking Canadian sisters could serve a predominantly Protestant and unchurched society that harbored anti-Catholic sentiments. To add to the complexities, there was the military base in Vancouver and across the Columbia River in Portland one of the region's rowdiest "tenderloin" districts.

Nonetheless, in their first year the sisters recorded impressive statistics that demonstrated their progress. They were boarding orphans, school children and homeless elderly. Day pupils also attended their school and in addition they had tended a number of sick persons in their homes.

Within a short time, the altruistic sisters were winning lay support from members of the commuity. In 1858, a group of 20 Vancouver women organized as the Ladies of Charity with the purpose of helping the Sisters of Providence to establish the Northwest's first hospital. Their membership included Jewish, Protestant and Catholic women who canvassed the community for donations. A member, Mary E. Biles, later wrote, "The work

In 1980, Mother Joseph's statue was erected in Statuary Hall in the nation's Capitol, where she and pioneer missionary, Marcus Whitman, are memorialized as Washington State's two most distinguished citizens. (Courtesy: Sisters of Providence Archives, Seattle, Washington)

met with the approval of everyone and all were willing to help us. Merchants gave of their ware; businessmen, cash; and mechanics, so many days labor." Biles said that the ladies held hops and balls to raise funds and on Thursdays, they "gathered in the sisters' parlors to transact business and sew by hand (sheets and comforters), as there were no sewing machines in Vancouver as yet."[8]

Military personnel from Fort Vancouver led girls at the academy in calisthenics. Designed by Mother Joseph, the building originally housed the academy, a hospital and the chapel. (Courtesy: Sisters of Providence Archives, Seattle, Washington)

At the Ladies of Charity's suggestion, Mother Joseph converted the combination laundry/bakery that she had just built into a four-bed ward. Biles reports that they named their hospital St. Joseph's in honor of its chief administrator and builder. Following a succession of temporary structures, the sisters in 1873 moved into their combination residence/academy/hospital which was three stories high and the largest brick building in Washington.

This was the first of 29 hospitals, academies, Indian schools and orphanages that Mother Joseph would design in her 46 years of service in the Northwest. Dressed in her long black habit with hammer and saw dangling from her belt, she insisted on personally supervising the construction of her buildings. A perfectionist, she climbed ladders to inspect rafters and bounced on beams to test their supports. At the age of 64, while superintending the construction of Sacred Heart Hospital in Spokane, she discovered an improperly laid chimney. The next morning, surprised workers found that she had dismantled and reconstructed it herself during the night. Popularly known as "the Builder," Mother Joseph was later recognized by the American Institute of Architects as the first architect of the Northwest.

From the start in the Vancouver hospital, the nuns took care of people, regardless of color, creed or ability to pay. In their continued efforts to help out, the Ladies of Charity often paid the dollar-a-day fee for indigent patients. However, the sisters soon realized that donations in Vancouver were not enough to finance the needed expansion they foresaw in the burgeoning Northwest.

They decided to embark on a unique fundraising venture. Taking younger nuns with her, Mother Joseph personally went on some of the first "begging tours" to mines in Montana and Idaho to appeal to lucky prospectors. Not only did the nuns go down into dark mining tunnels; they also told of outwitting stagecoach robbers, of spending weeks on horseback and camping outdoors, and of brushes with fire, wolves and even an angry grizzly bear.

Despite begging tours, donations and those patients who could afford to pay, the sisters struggled to make ends meet. In the records of Seattle's Providence Hospital, an 1888 entry reads, "I, the Chronicler, have lived here 11 years and I notice that although the hospital today seems prosperous, it was not always so. There were times when we did not know where to turn for help. In 1878—10 years ago—for three weeks once the house had only 25¢ to go on. . . ." A partial remedy was the Providence "ticket," a pioneer form of medical insurance which for $10 per year guaranteed full hospital coverage to its owner. The nuns found a ready market for their "tickets," especially among men in hazardous jobs, such as logging.

In their first hospitals, the nuns provided most of the care themselves with help from only a few non-professional staff members and volunteers. As their work load increased, they recognized a need for trained nurses. In 1889, they established the Northwest's first school of nursing at St. Vincent Hospital in Portland, followed by others in Washington. Admission requirements were non-sectarian, based only on a girl's moral character and ability to learn. The sisters relied on local doctors to help with instruction and hired a graduate from a prominent Eastern nursing school to head the program.

Prior to the turn of the century, the Sisters of Providence founded two dozen health care centers in the Northwest. Washington hospitals that Mother Joseph designed and built were: St. Joseph, Vancouver, 1858; Providence, Seattle, 1877; St. Mary, Walla Walla, 1880; Sacred Heart, Spokane, 1886; St. Peter, Olympia, 1887; St. John, Port Townsend, 1890; St. Elizabeth, Yakima, 1891; and St. Ignatius, Colfax, 1893. Responding to changing societal needs, the sisters have since closed some of their original facilities and have also established new ones. Throughout their history they have continued to modernize their facilities and programs to remain at the forefront of medical advancement.

Mother Joseph (left) joined other sisters on a "begging tour" to Montana mines. (Courtesy: Sisters of Providence Archives, Seattle, Washington)

Sister Peter Claver, past president of Spokane's Sacred Heart Medical Center, recently traced the development of women in health care from pioneer days to the present. She said, "Bedside care, pioneer doctoring, distribution of food and clothing, social service, home visits and attending the dying were women's ongoing tasks. From these have flowered schools of nursing, medical technology, dietetics, anesthesiology, medical records and a plethora of other health related professions where the majority of members have been women." In her opinion contemporary women emulate the "leadership, indefatigable stamina and commitment" of their forebears. She notes that Washington women have served in professional, management, technical and service roles, contributing to a quality of health care that "is equal to that of any found anywhere else in the country."[9]

Children's Orthopedic Hospital

Between 1890 and 1910, Seattle's population exploded from 42,837 to 237,174—more than quadrupling any other Washington city. Hospitals were full and new ones were under construction. For the city's poor it was a trying time and in terms of health care, only limited charitable assistance was available. Lacking nutritious diets, children of the poor were particularly vulnerable to outbreaks of typhoid, tuberculosis and dipththeria. However, as Anna Herr Clise discovered when her own son died of inflammatory rheumatism, even the wealthy found health care for children sadly inadequate. Seattle surgeons longed for a facility designed especially for children who required long-term care. At the time, child patients were placed in wards with adults.

Determined to improve the situation for others, Clise traveled East to inspect the Philadelphia Children's Hospital and to consult with her cousin who, as president of the American Medical Associaton, had established the hospital's ward for crippled children. On return home, she found that Washington state maintained facilities for blind, deaf and mentally ill children, but neglected those with other afflictions.

In early 1907, Clise invited 23 affluent Seattle women to meet with her at the Chamber of Commerce. Following her detailed report, each of the women contributed $20 to start a fundraising drive and launch an association that would never refuse help to a crippled child. The west coast's first Children's Orthopedic facility was a seven-bed ward at Seattle General Hospital where supportive surgeons volunteered to treat young patients. Clise and her friends did what they could to provide a nurturing environment and make the children comfortable. As the association evolved, the all-female board of trustees continued to handle administrative and financial matters, leaving medical treatment to the professional staff.

One of the first patients was four-year-old Julia B. who suffered from tuberculosis of the hips. After eight months of care, she was able to walk again. Her case and others proved that there was indeed hope for children suffering from such maladies as osteomyelitis, tuberculosis and emaciation, if sufficient rest and treatment were provided.

At one of its first meetings the board determined to care for children of minority races. Hospital historian Emilie Schwabacher said, "A newly formed association of black women, called the Dorcas Society, sought alliance with the women of COH. Action focused on Madelaine Black, a 14-year-old girl suffering from tuberculosis of the knee, and the two groups agreed to share Madelaine's expenses upon her admission to the children's ward."[10] By October, 1907, the trustees had established their fundamental and lasting policy of accepting any child, regardless of race, religion, or parents' ability to pay with the poor given first preference for treatment.

Initially, the community viewed the program with skepticism, questioning the motives of the "ladies bountiful." Parents hesitated to entrust sick children to their care. Not to be deterred, board members embarked on their own recruitment campaign, walking the streets on the lookout for crippled and malnourished children. Julia B. may well have been recruited when a trustee stopped her parents, explained the program, and urged them to accept hospital care at no cost. As the program began to win public confidence, young patients came from communities throughout the Northwest.

The trustees' energy was infectious and quickly spread into the community. A men's advisory committee, composed of business men and civic leaders, was organized to support the board and strengthen public confidence in the hospital. Board member Harriet Overton Stimson had a plan modeled after a hospital in Toronto, Canada, where a network of neighborhood groups lent its support. Local women responded enthusiastically to the concept and within a short time Orthopedic Guilds became a popular outlet for both social life and charity. The guilds organized effective and imaginative fundraising functions: "Kirmess," a carnival with extravagant stage shows by board and guild members, became a major Seattle social event; on "Hospital Sunday" guild members collected contributions made by area churches to COH; and there were "pound parties" where participants brought a pound of food for the hospital.

Snohomish County farmers quickly rallied to the "pound party," developing a tradition that eventually resulted in their contribution of 20 tons of produce and livestock which they brought to the hospital. Joining in,

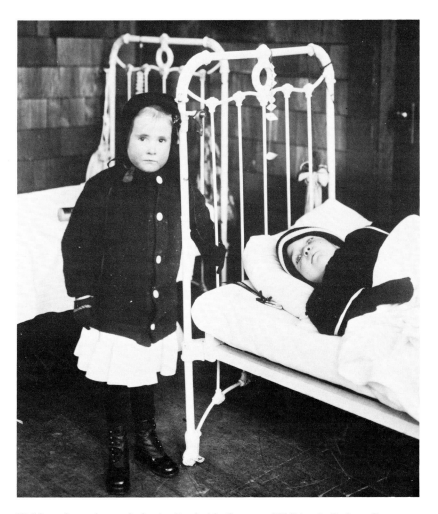

Children dressed warmly in the Fresh Air Cottage. (Children's Orthopedic Hospital and Medical Center Records, University of Washington Libraries)

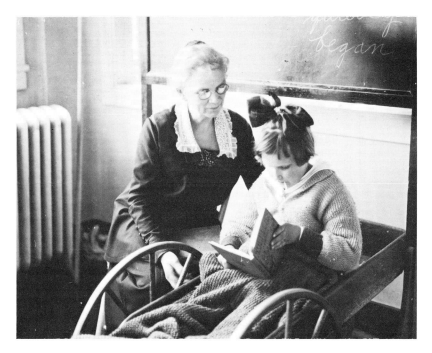

Having teacher's help, while your temperature is being taken. (Children's Orthopedic Hospital and Medical Center Records, University of Washington Libraries)

Snohomish children vied to see who could collect the most jars of jam and home-canned produce to add to the donation.

Due to long-term recovery periods, nursing was a vital component of the children's treatment, and COH was particularly responsive to the advancement of the nursing profession. On the recommendation of the medical staff, the board appointed Lillian Carter as Superintendent of the Hospital. Carter was instrumental in establishing a student nursing program and a visiting nurses' service for convalescent children.

In 1908, as a result of successful fundraising efforts, the association financed and built a 12-bed Fresh Air Cottage, followed in 1911 by a full scale 54-bed hospital, both located on Queen Anne Hill. The cornerstone laying was a major event, attracting the city's business, political and religious leaders. In her speech, Mrs. Clise made clear the trustees' intent, saying, " . . . This is not for our city alone but should and does reach out, offering help to the suffering children of the whole Northwest. . . ." Mayor George W. Dilling followed, saying "It is to the women of Seattle that we owe this great work and who are entitled to all credit for its projection and support. And it is safe in their hands. . . ."[11]

The new facilities created a cheerful environment with doctors, nurses, trustees and other volunteers working together to make recuperating children more comfortable. To accommodate young patients who frequently stayed for several months or even years, some of the trustees became teachers. As one young fellow put it in a letter to his pal, "If you think you can get out of school by coming here, you're fooled. The school comes right to you!"[12]

In 1920, the Seattle Community Chest was organized, a forerunner of today's United Way. Its purpose was to consolidate fundraising into an annual campaign that would benefit the city's member institutions, while protecting contributors from a constant barrage of requests. Envisioning relief from fund-drive pressures, COH guild members in Seattle wanted to participate. However, the trustees who regularly met with guilds throughout the state voted for the hospital to remain independent, thereby reaffirming its regional focus.

As emissaries of COH, guild members not only solicited donations; they were constantly on the lookout for patients, so that by 1920, the hospital had cared for children from 99 separate communities. In all parts of the state where people knew a family whose child had been helped, they rallied to support *their* hospital.

By the late 1940s, the trustees knew that they needed expanded facilities. The hospital was bursting at the seams with a postwar explosion of patients. Breakthroughs in medicine had given rise to several new departments that required space. COH was also beginning the long and complicated negotiations that would eventually lead to its affiliation with the University of Washington Medical School. Rather than remaining just a private charitable hospital, it was expanding to become a medical center for Northwest children.

Dorothy Stimson Bullitt, who was on the board and in the real estate business, chaired a committee that surveyed the city to determine the location of their new facility. In a still undeveloped part of Laurelhurst, she arranged to purchase 25 acres of land for $25,000. As president of the board, Frances Penrose Owen worked with another community leader, Paul Pigott, to steer a successful $3,500,000 campaign for the building fund.

Owen recalls the tremendous outpour of community involvement that rendered the complicated move cost free: "To move a hospital is not an easy job. The Far West Cab Company said they would transport all of the children and their nurses; the Teamsters Union offered to transport all of the equipment free." Volunteer workers gave up the previous weekend for a preliminary trial run, "so that they knew where all of the things were to go. We had every piece of equipment marked as to the floor and the location on the floor." Owen's conclusion is that "the City of Seattle has a heart!"

In the 1960s, COH responded to the social unrest that was sweeping the nation. Modeled after centers in Eastern cities, it established an outreach clinic for poor and minority children in Seattle's Central Area. Residents of the neighborhood and hospital representatives formed an advisory board to direct the project and to select personnel. Dr. Blanche Lavizzo was the first Medical Director of the Odessa Brown Clinic, named for the resident of the community who had brought the need for inner-city health care to public attention. According to Emilie Schwabacher, "A by-product . . . has been the acceptance of COH as a referral center for especially acute and complicated cases. The hospital 'out there' and seemingly inaccessible has become part of the health resource for the once remote inner city children."[13]

A recent name change to Children's Hospital and Medical Center reflects expanded objectives to treat all child ailments and to address all aspects of children's health care. Despite its growth and expansion, CHMC still gives the loving service that has always been its tradition. It remains a child-oriented facility directed by an all woman board.

Pure Food and Sanitation

In 1908, members of the General Federation of Women's Clubs were proud to have wielded a strong influence on Congress which enacted the long disputed Pure Food bill. In Washington State, clubwomen had successfully promoted similar legislation. Jennie Whitehead Ellis had chaired the Federation's national and statewide food sanitation committees. In her home town, Tacoma, she set forth to develop a model program.

With the new laws, clubwomen became self-appointed watchdogs to see that they were enforced. As president of Tacoma's Aloha Club, Ellis invited heads of other city women's organizations to her home where they formed a Pure Food Council. Thousands of women set to work garnering support from local doctors, the city health department, large grocery stores, church groups, the Tacoma News Tribune, and more. Soon Tacoma had its own city ordinance and at the women's urging, the mayor appointed a woman, Mary McCready, as food inspector. She was popular and competent, but resigned when a new administration took office.

Mayor A. W. Fawcett regarded the whole fuss about pure food as poppycock and said publicly that he had been eating all his life without the program and had not been poisoned yet. In compliance with the city's ordinance, he appointed Esther Allstrom, a woman who ran her own successful printing business. He reasoned that she would concentrate on making money, rather than on harassing food merchants. How wrong he was!

"Buy a Pencil!" Volunteers participate in one of many early fundraising campaigns at Children's Orthopedic Hospital.
(Children's Orthopedic Hospital and Medical Center Records, University of Washington Libraries)

Alstrom, a clubwoman who had been an outspoken suffragist, zealously tackled her new job. She enforced licensing requirements for food dealers, arresting those who failed to pay the required one dollar fee. On one occasion she ordered a vendor to destroy a barrel of tainted fish. When she later found it still on sale, she doused it with kerosene. Another marketeer ignored her order to move his display off the sidewalk, so she sawed off the legs of his table.

Because Mayor Fawcett's administration gave her no backing, Miss Allstrum resigned. Following his defeat in the next election, the Tacoma public demanded that the new mayor—a supporter of a clean city—reappoint her. She again set forth to educate merchants and buyers and to enforce the law. Tacoma's successful program received national attention. In Washington State, other cities including Spokane and North Yakima followed suit by appointing a woman as food inspector.

During the same period, Olympia's Janet Shotwell Moore was president of the State Federation of Women's Clubs. She had an aversion to the public drinking cup and towel that was a standard of public restrooms throughout the country. With her club sisters support, she headed a lobbying effort to demand that the legislature impose more sanitary conditions.

Doing their part, women's clubs in many Washington communities raised funds for the installation of public drinking fountains. In Bellingham and Puyallup, clubwomen successfully lobbied for ordinances to have townsfolk pen cattle, rather than allow them to roam the streets. Members of Bellingham's Aftermath Club pushed the city fathers to outlaw spitting on the streets and in streetcars.

Moore's successor as state president was Marion McCreadie of Sunnyside. During her term of office, she accepted Governor Hay's appointment to the state board of health where she served under successive administrations for 10 years. On a board subcommittee with her club sisters Janet Moore and Jennie Ellis, she successfully promoted legislation to establish county tuberculosis hospitals.

Coming from a rural community, McCreadie's concerns extended beyond larger urban areas. She addressed the Farmers' Institute of Sunnyside on the "Aim and Policy of the Modern Club Woman" which she said was to improve living conditions in rural areas, so that young people would want to stay there.

In subsequent years, Washington women have continued to support domestic concerns, such as hygiene, sanitation and public health. In the period around 1910, when women's suffrage became state law, women's groups were especially forceful, using their collective power to bring about reforms.

Notes

1. Oral history interview with Irene Shale, (1980), Washington Women's Heritage Project, University of Washington Manuscripts Collection.
2. *Told by the Pioneers,* vol. III, Washington Pioneer Project, Printed under WPA Sponsored Federal Project #5841, (1938), p. 168.
3. ibid. p. 159.
4. Anne C. Rafter, "The Pioneer Nurse," (King County, 1937). WPA Federal Writers' Project, History of Women in State Development, Washington State Historical Society.
5. ibid. Grace Coffman, "Women in Business and the Professions," (Pierce County, 1937).
6. Sisters of Providence Archives, Seattle.
7. ibid.
8. ibid. Mary E. Biles wrote her recollections for the archives in 1918.
9. Sister Peter Claver, Panelist on the History of Inland Empire Women and Health Care, "Women's Lives/Women's Stories" Conference (Spokane, 1987).
10. Emilie Schwabacher, *A Place for the Children* (Seattle: Children's Orthopedic Hospital and Medical Center, 1977), p. 7.
11. ibid. p. 21.
12. "The Hospital with a Smile," *Seattle Woman* I, 2 (June, 1923).
13. Schwabacher, p. 73.

Prior to World War II, Seattle hospital administrators refused to hire a trained nurse if she was black. The wartime emergency began to break down discriminatory barriers. These nurses, most of whom worked at Harborview Hospital, organized as the Mary Mahoney Club in 1943. (Courtesy of Esther Hall Mumford)

A farmer delivers a truck-load of apples to orphans at the Ryther Home. The petite, gray-haired woman in the middle is Mother Ryther. 1921. Photo by Asahel Curtis. (Courtesy of the Washington State Historical Society, Photo #42637)

Social Services: Institutions

4

From Washington's earliest history, women have shown their concern for orphaned children, unwed mothers, the elderly and other special groups of people. Native American women have a time-honored tradition of caring for extended families within their tribes. Catholic, Protestant, Jewish and Buddhist women organized within their respective denominations to lend a helping hand. Similarly, many a pioneer legend tells of women taking in orphans and sharing what they had with needy neighbors and wayfaring strangers.

During the 1880s, the transcontinental railroads reached Washington, connecting it with the East and infusing its communities with a population boom. During the same decade, women in the territory briefly claimed the ballot. Taking seriously both their rights and responsibilities as citizens, they began to form secular organizations to provide needed community services. At a time when charity donations came from individuals and when government assistance was unknown, the social service arena was wide open.

Whether local or part of a larger organization, Washington women's efforts were fueled by national activities. Suffragists, the Women's Christian Temperance Union and later the General Federation of Women's Clubs advocated reform and trumpeted the need for service agencies that could rescue and/or rehabilitate society's victims. By regarding the community as an extension of the home, women saw a logical connection between their social service and homemaking activities. Husbands, who would never have permitted their wives to work for pay, were often proud to support their volunteer work on behalf of a more livable community.

Women proceeded to found institutions to care for special populations including orphans, unwed mothers, young working women, the elderly and more. The following examples are representative of many others in communities throughout the state.

Orphan Homes

Like other early pioneers, Mrs. Ollie Ryther took it upon herself to care for orphans. Having left their farm in Iowa, Ryther and her husband came west in 1881 to build their cabin on the outskirts of Seattle. When a neighbor died, Mrs. Ryther adopted the four children and from that time on continued to take in any orphaned child that came her way. Her work gradually attracted community support and evolved into a Seattle institution, where during her lifetime she was mother to more than 3,100 children. Throughout the region, women organized a network of guilds to raise funds for the home.

Louisa Boren (left) and Mary Ann Boren Denny (right), wife of Seattle's founding father Arthur Denny, arrived on Puget Sound in 1851. As the city's first bride, Louisa married Arthur's brother, David. The philanthropic couple donated land for the "Orphan Home." (Courtesy of Special Collections Div., Univ. of Washington Libraries, UW Neg. #3810)

Mother Ryther had a talent for making do, even if her methods sometimes frustrated members of her board. She kept no records or reports and when the rent was due or supplies were scarce, she appealed to friends and businesses for help. Once when 25 of her charges needed shoes, she marched them into a shoe store and announced: "These children are staying here until you fit them all with shoes—that'll be your contribution to the Ryther Home."[1] In 1920, the people of Seattle built a large brick home for Mother Ryther and her "family," where after her death, a staff including four matrons continued the work that she had begun.

Groups of women in several Washington communities took a more conventional approach to organizing local charities. In 1884, 15 Seattle women got together to organize the Ladies' Relief Society. Founders included Sarah Yesler, Babette Schwabacher Gatzert, Caroline Sanderson and Mary Leary all of whom were early pioneers and wives of leading community businessmen. Their hearts went out to destitute people who roamed the rutted city streets. At first, board members opened their homes to provide temporary relief to the poor regardless of creed, nationality or color.

Within a year, the trustees narrowed their focus and determined to build a home especially for orphans and abandoned mothers with small children. They successfully persuaded the county commissioners to allocate $15 per month for each child and raised funds to build the "Orphan Home" on land donated by Seattle founders David and Louisa Boren Denny.

The board established a kindergarten for children too young to attend school. Meals were simple, but nutritious, with meat supplied once a day and pies and cakes "utterly forbidden." The children wore clothing that was "plain, simple, clean, and neat." While local doctors volunteered to provide medical service, members of the community organized recreational outings for the children. Relief funds left over from Seattle's great fire of 1889 eventually enabled the Society to move to a new brick building on a 15-acre campus where it changed its name to the Seattle Children's Home.

Like Seattle, downtown Spokane burned to the ground in 1889. Lillie Ross's friends rallied to her idea of forming a Ladies' Benevolent Society to establish a home for the indigent. As a fundraiser, Spokane's elite held a ball in the Van Dorn Opera House with some of the proceeds earmarked for the Society. Spokane's first charity prompted an outpouring of public and private support. At first the Society housed both the elderly and children, but later narrowed its focus to become the Spokane Children's Home. To assist mothers slim of purse, the board also organized a Women's Exchange for the sale of homemade items, especially food and needle work.

In the same year, a group of Tacoma women founded and built their Children's Industrial Home which included separate gymnasiums for boys and girls, along with flower and vegetable gardens for the orphans to maintain. Among the early board members were Jane Crombie Bradley who had spent her childhood in an old-time institutional orphanage and Ruby Chapin Blackwell whose adoptive parents had run one of Tacoma's first hotels. Knowing what it meant for a child to be separated from its natural parents, these women helped shape the family atmosphere that prevailed in the home.

Homes for "Fallen Women"

At the root of the orphan problem was a lax moral climate. Proper townsfolk avoided saloons and brothels, branding the gambler, drunkard or unwed mother a social outcast. During their brief foray as voters, Washington women had attempted to clean up their cities, but with their loss of the ballot in 1887, vice once again reigned triumphant.

Children play on "the community swing" at the Seattle Children's Home on Queen Anne Hill, ca. 1919. (Courtesy of the Seattle Children's Home).

Members of the Western Washington Women's Christian Temperance Union readily endorsed a proposal by Maude E. Turrell of Tacoma to open a "home for fallen women." They had hoped for statewide sponsorship so that their institution could receive governmental support, but the Eastern Washington Union, primarily because of geographic distance, decided not to participate.

Located in Tacoma, the White Shield Home began in temporary quarters, admitting its first unwed mothers and their infant children in 1889. Donations came from the local business community and from WCTU units throughout western Washington, so that in 1892 the program moved into its own spacious residence overlooking Puget Sound. The Home's stated purpose was "to redeem our erring sister from her life of shame into a life of pure, true womanhood, by surrounding her with the influence, comfort and Christian teaching of a home. She whose peculiar sin shuts her out from any other home, can find shelter here till she can prove her worthiness to take her place again in the world as a woman and not as an outcast."[2]

The W.C.T.U.'s White Shield Home for fallen women. The 1892 annual report describes its setting "in beautiful Prospect Park—a most desirable residence portion of Tacoma commanding a wide view of Puget Sound, of the Olympic range, and an unsurpassed view of that peak—unrivaled in grandeur, our mountain [Mt. Rainier]." (Courtesy of the Tacoma Public Library).

In northwest Native American tribes, there was no orphan problem, since with large, extended families, there was always an aunt or a grandmother to take in a child who's mother had died. Children were often raised by their grandparents, while their parents worked. Here members of the Nez Perce Woman's Industrial Society pose with teacher Kate McBeth, right. The Nez Perce Reservation is just across the Idaho border from Clarkston. (Courtesy of the Spokane Public Library, Northwest Room)

Following meetings with New York evangelist Charles Crittenton in 1899, women in Spokane and Seattle organized homes with a similar purpose. In memory of his daughter who died at age four, Crittenton had founded a mission in 1883 to rescue the unwed mother, the battered or abandoned wife and their babies. With support from local businesses, the boards in Seattle and Spokane established commodious, comfortable homes, complete with park-like grounds, obstetrical wards and later day nurseries to assist working mothers.

In addition to rescue work, Crittenton, like the W.C.T.U., emphasized prevention. During his 1899 visit, he established Florence Crittenton Purity Circles in Dayton, Walla Walla and Colfax. They engaged in fundraising to support the nearest home, canned home-grown produce and sewed for the inmates. Like the Circles in Spokane and Seattle, they organized mothers' meetings and distributed literature to young girls, warning them of the perils of society. Both the W.C.T.U. and the Circles sent members to visit local jails and red light districts, where they told prostitutes about the home and urged them to reform.

The Florence Crittenton Homes not only cared for girls in their "hour of need;" staff members and volunteers also provided counseling, child care instruction and vocational training to prepare the young mother for her return to society. Whenever possible, the homes helped her to find a respectable position, so that she could later support herself and her child. Track records of former inmates at the homes recorded many success stories, along with poignant accounts of some who went "back to the life from which we tried so hard to save them."[3]

In Spokane, Al and May Arkwright Hutton contributed generously to both the Spokane Children's Home and the Florence Crittenton Home. Raised by her blind, paternal grandfather in Ohio, May had not forgotten her roots as an illegitimate child; nor had Al whose childhood home had been an institutional orphanage. The hardships that they had known always motivated the Huttons to do whatever they could to help the orphaned child and the unwed mother.

As a member of the Crittenton board, May related easily to the clients, taking a personal interest in their welfare and offering some creative—if unorthodox—alternatives for keeping mother and child together. Unlike other women on the board, May was from a working class background and could realistically anticipate the hardships a single working mother would have to face. She shared the board's commitment to sending the young

Under the leadership of President Harriet Parkhurst, the Seattle Florence Crittenton Rescue Circle raised funds to purchase this building with 27 rooms and several acres of grounds about six miles south of the city. Originally, it was the Seattle Baptist University, a seminary for women. Photo by Asahel Curtis. (Courtesy of Special Collections Div., Univ. of Washington Libraries, A. Curtis Photo #5330)

woman on to a decent job. However, in her opinion, the ideal arrangement was for her to go to a home and husband of her own.

Having worked as a cook for miners, May Hutton understood lonely men. In her chauffeur-driven Thomas Flyer, she went for rides in the Palouse country, seeking out farmers who had little contact with marriageable women and who longed for the companionship of a wife and family. Playing cupid, she arranged meetings and after a few months, if her instincts had been right, Al would give the bride away at a wedding ceremony held before the fireplace in the Hutton's parlor. As a follow-up, May occasionally dropped in on the families to pay a friendly visit and make sure that all was well.

Hutton Settlement. With their stately brick homes in the background, these boys prepare the field-sized garden, where they raise some of the "family's" produce. (Courtesy of the Eastern Washington State Historical Society, Spokane)

Children's Homes: Then and Now

Following May's death, Al carried on their benevolent mission by founding the Hutton Settlement, a cluster of well-constructed brick homes for orphans, located in a sylvan setting just east of Spokane. As in a normal family, a married couple headed each household; the husband went to work at a regular job; the wife stayed home, cooked meals, did housework, and cared for her children. Al wanted the orphans' upbringing to be as natural as possible, free of the vestiges of the institutions he had known.

During the remainder of his life and in his will, he provided millions of dollars for the Hutton Settlement, while turning over the administration to a strong board of civic-spirited women. Agnes Cowley Paine, daughter of early Spokane missionaries, was the first president of the board. Her daughter, Margaret Paine Cowles, a three-term president who still serves on the board, continues to take an active interest in the children and in their day-to-day routines. She recalls earlier times when board members met regularly at the Settlement to do whatever needed to be done, including sewing and canning—until the Board of Health put a stop to the activity.

Today the Hutton Settlement is one of Washington's few remaining orphanages. Some of the older institutional homes have been converted to other child-oriented purposes. The century-old Seattle Children's Home is a comprehensive mental health center for psychiatrically impaired chil-

The Reverend Harrison and Libby Beach Brown, founders of the Children's Home Society of Washington. (Courtesy of the Children's Home Society of Washington)

dren, while the Ryther Child Center treats severely to moderately disturbed children. Like institutional orphanages, cloistered homes for unwed mothers are a thing of the past.

In the 1890s, when many Washington communities treated their orphanage as their favorite charity, Libby Beach Brown began canvassing the state to promote a controversial alternative. A trained social worker, Brown and her husband the Reverend Harrison Brown had been commissioned nationally to found a statewide Children's Home Society in Washington. Due to financial pressures, the Reverend Brown initially accepted a pastorate in Seattle while his wife carried forth their mission. Rather than place a child in an orphanage or on a poor farm, the Society moved its charges from temporary receiving homes into suitable adoptions in families.

The Reverend Brown later wrote, "Mrs. Brown was a fluent and interesting speaker and drew to the support of the society many people of intelligence and high standing in different parts of the state and her executive ability enabled her to organize and establish local advisory boards

In 1910, "Alpha," an orphan in Yakima, came to the attention of black women in Seattle's Dorcas Charity Club. The club worked with the Children's Home Society to arrange for a member, Lillie LaFon, to adopt the child. (Courtesy of Black Heritage Society of Washington State.)

which became a network of activity covering the entire state. . . . The contributions slowly increased and the children multiplied in our hands."[4]

The Browns themselves began to practice what they preached as soon as they moved to Seattle, making their own home an initial receiving home for unwanted children. Their first child was Cassie, a little girl so weak and undernourished that she could not walk and had to be carried. Libby Brown later reported that Cassie "had grown to beautiful womanhood" with her adoptive Seattle parents.[5] As the society grew and established temporary receiving homes throughout the state, Cassie's story was often repeated.

Following Libby Brown's term, her husband and other men dominated the board of directors for decades. Women continued to serve as the primary care givers and case workers who arranged permanent homes for orphaned children. As members of the network of auxiliaries that Libby Brown promoted, women have been mainstays of the Society's financial support.

Modern statewide services—including government social welfare programs and the Children's Home Society of Washington—stress family counselling to counter problems and where possible to preserve natural parent-child relationships. There are several temporary shelters and services to assist victims of domestic violence. In the case of orphans, temporary foster care and the arrangement of a suitable adoption are today's preferred methods. Organizations such as the Seattle Milk Fund and Bellevue's Overlake Services League (both outgrowths of the Seattle Ladies' Fruit and Flower Mission founded in 1914) provide assistance to families, often enabling them to weather hard times and remain together.

Criminal Justice

A priority of the W.C.T.U. was the revamping of the criminal justice system, especially regarding its treatment of women and children. As inmates, the prostitute and the homeless child were at the heart of the issue. The Washington State Legislature responded in 1893 by passing a Police Matron Bill, but in most Washington cities, women accused of crimes continued to be searched by men, thrown in jail with male prisoners and guarded by men. Similarly, children were commonly treated as adults, despite the existence of laws to establish juvenile courts.

Bolstered by the ballot in 1910, which the W.C.T.U. referred to as "our weapon," clubwomen in Spokane, Seattle and other Washington cities saw to it that jail matrons were appointed. They also successfully agitated for children's courts with separate quarters and counselors for juvenile offenders.

As president of the State Federation of Women's Clubs, Janet Shotwell Moore of Olympia personally inspected the reformatory for boys and girls at Chehalis. On the recommendation of the clubs, Governor Lister appointed a commission of women, chaired by Moore, to develop plans for sex-segregated facilities. The commission selected a site at Grand Mound in Thurston County for the Maple Lane School for Wayward Girls which opened in 1914. As a follow-up, the WSFWC urged the governor to appoint a commission with at least two women as members to supervise state institutions dealing with women and children.

In the 1920s, State Representative Belle Reeves sponsored a bill to move women from the State Prison at Walla Walla to their own facility. With support from Reba Hurn in the Senate, she pushed the bill through both houses of the legislature, only to have it vetoed by the governor. It was the 1970s, before a similar bill became law, resulting in the establishment of the women's reformatory at Purdy.

The Spokane Police Department hired Nora Hudspeth as the matron in charge of women prisoners in 1913. Women's clubs had promoted the establishment of the new position to give female prisoners—previously guarded by men—some protection and privacy. (Courtesy of the Eastern Washington State Historical Society, Spokane, Photo #L34–36.39)

The Young Women's Christian Association

For some, the recessionary 1890s were not so gay. Struggling families on rural homesteads reluctantly sent their daughters—sometimes as young as 12—to Washington's larger cities in hopes that they could find a paying job and help the folks back home. Penniless and alone, the girls were easy prey for "white slavers" who readily offered them work in local brothels.

Realizing the girls' need for a safe haven and remembering her experience in Washington, D.C., Mrs. Rees Daniels called together 27 Seattle women to form a local chapter of the Young Women's Christian Association. The YWCA's membership was open to every moral girl or woman, irrespective of religious faith; it was a friend to any woman who asked for assistance; and its ultimate objective was to help working women toward self support.

During the last quarter of the 19th century, chapters of the organization blossomed throughout the United States. The YWCA quickly gained footing in several Washington cities and in student chapters on college campuses. Joining the national board were Tacoma's Anna Mary Holbrook Weyerhaeuser, Seattle's Lucy Langdon Burwell and Walla Walla's Mary Shipman Penrose who in 1913 was elected to a two-year term as national president.

A Friend of the Working "Girl"

The Seattle association's beginnings were typical of other Washington YWCAs. In a downtown storeroom, donated by Mary Shorey, volunteers created a comfortable lounge and the city's first cafeteria which served 10¢ lunches to working girls.[6] The board soon hired a trained YWCA secretary who came west from Missouri to manage the association and provide employment and counseling services.

Employers were just beginning to hire women for nontraditional jobs in offices and in factories. Among the YWCA's early programs was health and fitness, originally designed for the working girl who needed strength to operate unwieldy industrial or office equipment—including the turn-of-the-century typewriter. Within a short time members were enjoying physical exercise for both health and recreational purposes.

Members of the Seattle YWCA paraded down Fourth Avenue in their 1913 whirlwind campaign to raise $400,000 for a new building. They sang campaign songs and waved at onlookers, while riding in style in 100 autos provided by the Seattle Taxicab Company. (YWCA of Seattle/King County Records, University of Washington Libraries)

Seattle YWCA President Emma Wallingford Wood and other board members join in the ground breaking ceremony in 1914. The annual report described the building as "An eight story Class A structure, pronounced the best of its kind in the country, excepting the national building headquarters in New York City." (YWCA of Seattle/King County Records, University of Washington Libraries)

Board members of the Tacoma YWCA raise funds for a new building in the 1920s. Anna Mary Holbrook Weyerhaeuser donated money to build and equip Weyerhaeuser Hall, a part of the structure that has a commanding view of Commencement Bay. (Courtesy of the Tacoma Public Library)

Traveler's Aid

Among the first supporters of the Northwest YWCAs were the transcontinental railroads who assisted with salaries for depot matrons. At Tacoma's Union Depot, Harriet Ellis's job was to guard and guide young women and children traveling alone. While Ellis worked the day shift, Mary Weingarten took over at night. The Traveler's Aid Society was founded by women after the 1893 World's Columbian Exposition in Chicago, when thousands of girls allegedly disappeared. It began locally as a YWCA program and later spun off as an independent agency.

Clubs for Girls and Women

Washington's YWCAs organized a variety of clubs to keep young women and girls "interested in the best things and thereby prevent their being attracted by questionable amusements."[7] There were occupational clubs for office workers, factory workers, domestic workers and professional women (in Seattle, the forerunner of the Business and Professional Women's Club). High school girls in Pierce County and Bellingham and later throughout the state donned middies and blue skirts to become Girl Reserves, while younger girls joined Bluebird or Rainbow Clubs.

Mary Shipman Penrose, wife of the president of Whitman College, by the bridge leading to the president's home. (1926) According to her daughter, Frances Owen, she was educated in the East and came to Walla Walla on her wedding trip in 1896. "She had never seen a town like it, but had a talent for adapting, and she didn't lose her contacts in the East." Along with her presidency of the national YWCA board, she helped establish a Walla Walla branch and a campus YWCA at Whitman, where students affectionately called her "Mother Penrose." (Courtesy of Northwest and Whitman College Archives, Penrose Library)

Members of the Seattle YWCA's Cosmopolitan Club pose with a variety of athletic equipment in the gymnasium. (YWCA of Seattle/King County Records, University of Washington Libraries)

The Cosmopolitan Club drew local women into world fellowship activities. There were also clubs for ethnic women. Seattle listed junior and senior Japanese, Chinese, Russian and Culture (for black women) clubs. In Spokane, Scandinavian immigrants who worked as domestics during the day came to the YWCA for evening English classes and friendship.

Members of each club met for weekly dinners, entertainment, classes and intramural athletic events. They also looked forward to summer camp which in the early days was often held at a beach cottage that someone let them use.

Seattle's Eight-story Building

By the early 1900s, the Seattle association knew that it needed a building of its own. Following the example of Portland's YWCA, it determined that prior to canvassing businessmen, it would seek contributions from working women throughout the city. When Seattle's eight-story downtown building opened in 1914, President Emma Wallingford Wood proudly announced that the association was debt-free, having paid its $400,000 bill in cash.

In a later fundraising speech to a somewhat skeptical Seattle Rotary Club, YWCA Secretary Emily Southmayd explained that the operation of the building was paid for "by the cafeteria, the hotel, the Turkish baths,

Intramural basketball was a popular sport, organized in many Washington communities by the YWCA. Here, Skagit County teams vie in spirited competition. (Courtesy of the Skagit County Historical Museum).

and the tea room, so that these rooms must not be regarded as an extravagant provision for the poor girl."[8] She emphasized that the building's "luxuries" provided income, generated by fees from members and guests who used them, and that outside contributions continued to support welfare work, performed largely for non-members in need of temporary shelter, guidance and employment assistance.

Vocational Training Programs

In 1914, when the legislature enacted a landmark $10.00 per week minimum wage for working women, YWCAs throughout the state focused their energies on vocational training and placement. They offered classes in millinery, dressmaking, housekeeping, cafeteria work, practical nursing, salesmanship and more, so that girls would have the qualifications for a desirable job.

Through the years, YWCA employment services had developed rapport with local businesses, working to meet their needs and to arrange job placements for clients. In addition they had promoted better conditions for women in the workplace. Seattle's Bemis Brothers Bag Factory is an example of a company that established a comfortable women's lounge and morning and afternoon work breaks in response to requests from the YWCA. Like other cooperative companies, it sponsored athletic teams and also welcomed YWCA teachers who came to the work site to offer informal classes during the lunch hour.

Another early YWCA program was home economics, designed to prepare girls for marriage or for work as cooks, domestics or nursemaids. In Seattle, mothers could leave young children in the nursery so that they could participate. In a mileau that frowned on a married woman working for pay if her husband could afford to support her, the 1914 class schedule read, "Home making occupies a leading place in the schedule of this school, for this is not a simple kind of knowledge that can be left to chance, it is a serious many-sided study brimful of opportunity to apply the highest kind of knowledge, science and art, and all the ideals of culture and education."

Matrons with the age-old complaint that "good help is hard to find," often hired a maid and then enrolled her in the program. To facilitate a harmonious working relationship, the YWCA offered additional courses for matrons, teaching them reasonable expectations and respect for their maid's rights. As word spread about Washington's minimum wage and eight-hour day statutes, young women flocked to the state from all parts of the nation. In periods of high unemployment, domestic work (not covered by the law),

Organized locally in 1918, Girl Reserves Clubs pose for a photo on the roof of the Seattle YWCA building. Their watch words were "Health, Knowledge, Service, and Spirit." (YWCA of Seattle/King County Records, University of Washington Libraries)

was often the only available option. The YWCA's program helped and membership in the Domestic Workers' Union swelled. In addition to giving the girls training and placement services, the YWCA and their union gave them social and educational resources for their free time.

The "Center for Colored Girls"

By 1919, the Seattle YWCA's Culture Club, under the leadership of Mrs. W. D. Carter, established its own Phillis Wheatley Branch in the heart of the black community. The "center for colored girls" became the first of its kind in the Northwest, providing social, educational and employment programs, as well as overnight accommodations for out-of-town girls. "We teach the girls, whatever they do to do it well," said Carter. "When they do that they remove the prejudice against our race. . . . Already this association has created a better feeling among our people."[9]

Like churches, the branch became a public meeting place in the black community and as such hosted weddings, dances for young people and meetings for black women's clubs. According to Bertha Pitts Campbell, who was active in the branch in the 1920s, the city's racial climate may have benefited, because in spite of some difficulties, "the 'Y' always listened." In other Washington YWCAs—notably Olympia, Tacoma and Spokane—black women also participated, making progress toward interracial understanding long before the Civil Rights Movement brought the issue to the attention of the larger public.

Campbell recalls some of the hurdles that she encountered and that were typical not only in the Northwest but throughout the nation. Black women could swim in the YWCA pool only on Saturday afternoon—before it was cleaned and drained. When Seattle black women first established their branch, they sent a non-voting representative to board meetings at the downtown YWCA. In the 1930s, when Campbell became the branch representative, she protested, saying that if she was expected to attend meetings, then she demanded the right to vote just like everyone else. The Seattle board presented the issue to the national board which granted its approval, making Bertha Campbell the first black woman to vote on a YWCA board and making the Seattle chapter the first integrated association in the United States.

Since the 1920s, when Community Chests (a forerunner of United Way) made their debut in Washington communities, YWCAs have been charter beneficiaries. As a consequence, they gradually deemphasized earlier social clubs and membership activities that had helped with fundraising. Today YWCAs continue to serve women and families throughout the state. They offer coeducational health and fitness classes, employment services for teens and adults, day care for children of working parents, emergency shelter for abused and homeless women and their families, and in some cases low cost residential or hotel accommodations for women.

Settlement House: A Haven for Immigrants

Between 1880 and the first World War, waves of non-English speaking European refugees were coming to Washington—among them Russian and Polish Jews who had been persecuted, denied an education, and ultimately forced to leave their homeland. The Northwest's early pioneers already included educated European Jews who had emigrated to the *goldeneh Medinah* (land of gold) in search of a better life. Many had come as families,

Northwest YWCAs hold their convention at Seabeck in 1917. (YWCA of Seattle/King County Records, University of Washington Libraries)

66

Rose Lu Soun and her friends organized a Seattle Chinese Girl Reserves unit which in 1923 performed traditional music and dance at the Helig Theater to raise funds for famine relief in China. (YWCA of Seattle/King County Records, University of Washington Libraries)

Esther Levy (left) who in 1889 called together 37 women to organize Seattle's Ladies' Hebrew Benevolent Society was succeeded by her daughter, Lizzie Cooper (right), as president of the board. To perpetuate their wives' names, Aubrey Levy and his son-in-law business partner, Isaac Cooper, established a trust in support of needy children and their families. They also left sizable bequests to the Jewish Family and Child Services, the Caroline Kline Galland Home for the Aged, and Children's Orthopedic Hospital. Here Lizzie Cooper poses with her husband on their wedding day. (Courtesy of Special Collections Div., Univ. of Washington Libraries, Negative #1104 and Negative #1106)

gravitating to communities where they established businesses and became involved in social, political and cultural activities. Among them was Bailey Gatzert who was elected Seattle's mayor in 1875. His wife was Babette Schwabacher whose brothers and their families pioneered in Walla Walla, Dayton and Colfax. Babette was instrumental in establishing the Seattle Section of the Council of Jewish Women, founded nationally in 1893 for the purpose of non-sectarian community service and education.

Sensitive to the plight of new immigrants, the Seattle Council determined to found a facility modeled after Jane Addams's Hull House in Chicago. Babette Gatzert and her friends founded their first Settlement House in Seattle's central area in 1906, offering instruction in English, Americanization, sewing, and religion.

In 1910, they constructed the Deaconess Settlement House in the Rainier Valley to serve a rapidly growing population of Italian immigrants. With the opening of the Panama Canal in 1914, they prepared for a new influx of émigrés escaping from the war-torn Balkans in Eastern Europe.

By this time, their original Settlement House had become a valuable resource for the entire neighborhood and its clientele had expanded to include the native poor. The trustees added employment services, youth programs, legal advice, and literary and social clubs. To further encourage education, they awarded an annual scholarship to the University of Washington, thereby honoring one of the neighborhood's most talented young people.

Since most of the homes in the vicinity lacked bathrooms, Settlement House provided free baths. From the start, doctors and nurses volunteered to provide gratuitous medical treatment. When the baby clinic was later established in 1912, trained nurses joined the paid staff, although doctors continued to donate their services.

Transition to Education Center

Expanded programs required expanded space. In 1916, the community celebrated the opening of a fully-equipped new building which *The Jewish Voice* dubbed "a monument to women's energy." A year after it opened, the trustees changed the building's name to the Education Center, which in their opinion more closely defined its revised purpose.

Through the years women on the board continued to add new programs. Having helped to establish the King County Juvenile Court, Mina Eckstein worked to develop guidance and support programs for troubled youth. Other board members persuaded Nellie Cornish to open a branch of her school at the Center, where with help from members of the Ladies' Musical Club, they added folk dancing and music to the curriculum.

In their early history, members of the Seattle Council of Jewish Women founded additional service agencies, including the Caroline Kline Galland Home for the Aged and the Ladies' Hebrew Benevolent Society (later named Jewish Family and Child Services) which assisted needy families.

Today's Neighborhood House

In later years, trustees of the Education Center again changed the name of their agency—this time to Neighborhood House—which today maintains three child care centers and five community centers, bringing needed services to the poor in their own Seattle neighborhoods. As in Seattle, Jewish women in other Washington communities have responded to the needs of the poor, the aged, the immigrant and more, establishing numerous agencies to lend a helping hand.

Notes

1. *Seattle Times* (June 16, 1946), Magazine Section.
2. Western Washington W.C.T.U., Annual Meeting Reports, 1889.
3. ibid.
4. Rev. H. D. Brown, *History of the Washington Children's Home Society,* n.d., unpub., Children's Home Society of Washington, Seattle.
5. "Washington Children's Home Finder" (Seattle, Jul, 1910), vol. 14, #2.
6. Through the 1920s and 1930s, single working women were called "girls." They were referred to as "women" when they married and when, if possible, they left a paid job to become a homemaker. For a wife whose husband could afford to support her, voluntary commitments were laudible; but to accept a paying job could have constituted an insult to the husband.
7. Emily Southmayd, YWCA of Seattle/King County Records, University of Washington Libraries, n.d.
8. "Rotary Club at YWCA," *Argus* (Mar. 10, 1917).
9. "Colored Branch of YWCA opened after Long Effort," *Seattle Post-Intelligencer* (Aug. 31, 1919).

Grace Turner of the Spokane Public Library staff in World War I uniform with co-workers who served as Red Cross volunteers. This was the poster for the library's campaign to collect books to send to doughboys abroad. Ca. 1918. (Courtesy of the Spokane Public Library, Northwest Room).

Social Services—Outreach

5

In the previous chapter, the focus was on institutions and community centers to which clients came for service. This chapter deals with organizations with a similar mission which train volunteers to reach out into the community. There is admittedly some overlap. For example, the W.C.T.U. and the Florence Crittenton Rescue Circles, as already indicated, offered institutional care with professional staff, while simultaneously training volunteers to advocate and to extend a helping hand in the community. Outreach organizations discussed in this chapter have a broad mission that frequently extends beyond social services into the arts, education, health care and other areas presented in other parts of the book.

The American Red Cross

"Remember the Maine" was the rallying cry of Seattle women who attended a public meeting in June, 1898, to organize civilian support for American troops going to war against Spain. The women responded enthusiastically when Mary B. Brainerd, a close friend of Clara Barton, suggested forming a Red Cross Society. Groups in other Washington communities soon followed suit, collecting supplies and shipping them to soldiers stationed in the United States, Cuba and the Philippines. Brainerd

later recalled, "There was much to do as the nine transports which sailed from Puget Sound received their last American cheers from us."[1]

Having witnessed the work of the International Red Cross during the Franco-Prussian War, Barton had founded the American Red Cross in 1881. By a later Congressional mandate, the agency was charged with providing relief to disaster victims and with serving as a vehicle of communication between United States civilians and their Army and Navy. In time of war, it was to care for the wounded and perform other duties in accord with the Geneva Convention.

With the end of the Spanish-American War, several local Red Cross units disbanded. A few in western Washington turned their attention to disaster relief, sending aid to victims of the San Francisco earthquake in 1906 and to famine sufferers in China in 1907.

The United States' entry into the Great War in 1917 to "make the world safe for democracy" galvanized unprecedented activity. Members of the General Federation of Women's Clubs, the D.A.R., the P.E.O. and church guilds considered it their patriotic duty to join the Red Cross. In communities all over Washington, Red Cross volunteers mustered at a furious pace to organize sewing circles, canteens, motor corps, Liberty Loan campaigns, nursing departments and more.

A group of Seattle women meets to crochet bandages and knit odds and ends for soldiers during World War I. Pictured are Elma Collins (Lisle), Katherine Kittinger, Marion Baillie (Tomkins), and Gladys Waterhouse (Minor). (Courtesy of the Seattle/King County Chapter of the American Red Cross).

The Spokane Chapter—with branches and auxiliaries in 13 rural counties—shipped carloads of bacon, apples and flour to war-ravaged France for civilian relief. Volunteers in Vancouver borrowed trucks from the military post to haul high quality sphagnum moss from which they made absorbent dressings. In the country town of Daisy, where ice was still a rarity, Red Cross volunteers borrowed all of the freezers they could find; farm women donated cream; stores supplied sugar and ice cream powder; boys volunteered to turn the cranks; and the treat was sold at evening socials as a fundraiser.

Kittitas County's Jean C. Davidson mustered the Minute Women to recruit at least one Red Cross volunteer from each household. With the county divided into neighborhood round tables, women met to sew garments and to assemble "housewives" (containing needles, safety pins, darning cotton, buttons and scissors) and "comfort bags" (with soap, toothpaste, post cards, etc.), to send to the troops. The D.A.R. launched a statewide campaign, urging ladies to pledge themselves to donate a 5¢ bar of Ivory soap and a tube of toothpaste per month.

Seattle's Dorothy Stimson Bullitt remembers her disappointment at the beginning of the war, when she wanted to join her friend Tippi Kittinger and go to Europe "where the action was." Her father C. D. Stimson, who was head of the Pacific Northwest region of the Red Cross, said, "No," and suggested that she volunteer her services locally by organizing a Red Cross

On a farm near Ritzville, Martha Knox Dorman—pioneer mother of seven and a grandmother—knits socks to donate to the Red Cross. Her granddaughter, Mildred Chargois Tanner, recalls that she received letters from soldiers in France, thanking her for the soft socks that were much more comfortable than those made by less experienced knitters. (Courtesy of Mildred Chargois Tanner)

Motor Brigade. From her downtown office, she recruited friends, each of whom had a telephone and a car. Dubbed the "swiftest transportation in Seattle," the motor corp taxied soldiers and sailors, wartime visitors, goods made by sewing circles, and more from one end of town to the other.

On his way home from Washington, D.C., Stimson arrived in Spokane at the same time as a troop train—one of four that passed through the city on the same day. Members of the canteen department had made their usual preparations with urns of hot coffee, sandwiches, doughnuts, Adams Pure California Fruit Chewing Gum, apples, magazines, cigarettes, post cards and flowers. Among the volunteers were women from the Dorcas Society

Members of the Seattle Motor brigade pose in front of the Volunteer Park conservatory in 1917. Their uniforms consisted of a gray serge, knee-length tailored coat, riding trousers, a round gray cap with the Red Cross insignia, brown leather puttees and brown leather belts. (Courtesy of the Seattle/King County Chapter of the American Red Cross)

to care for soldiers of color. When the troops tumbled off the train, the primly uniformed hostesses were ready to greet and serve them.

A first-aid nurse, Nellie E. Toms, was on hand to dress the wounds of two injured recruits. One had suffered a head wound in a badly negotiated attempt to pass from one car to another, while the other had crushed his hand in a fall from an upper berth. Stimson, who had arrived on the scene unexpectedly, was particularly interested in the first-aid work. He gave high praise to the local canteen as the best demonstration of any he had seen on his way across the continent.

The Spokane workers, who sometimes met 15 trains a day, received letters of thanks and friendship from all over the United States and abroad. Recruits frequently observed that the Spokane canteen was the only one on their way across the continent to offer to stamp and send their mail. Edith D. Smith, a canteen volunteer, later recalled, "We went around with stamped postcards, for we always wanted the boys to write them."[3] When the troops reboarded their train, the women gave them flowers.

As discussed in the chapter on health care, Red Cross nursing departments had their hands full, caring for wounded soldiers and civilian victims of the virulent influenza epidemic of 1918. Assisting them were sewing departments which made surgical shirts, pajamas, bandages and flu masks. Canteen workers did their part by delivering meals to make-shift hospitals and private homes.

Members of the Colored Red Cross pose with soldiers at Fort Lewis in 1917. LeEtta King later reflected: "Times changed with the War. You didn't have so much fun. You worked, and the girls formed groups to entertain the soldiers. One of the groups that I was a member of became affiliated with the Red Cross. Now there was discrimination with the Red Cross group. . . .We made bandages and that sort of thing but we weren't just really a part of the whole Red Cross movement. We were in a little unit of our own, but we knew this separation, this discrimination somehow. Why it would be with the Red Cross, I don't know. You see, at that time the soldiers were not integrated, so we were supposed to be working for our boys, and that made a difference somehow. . . ."[3] After the War the Seattle group disassociated itself from the Red Cross to form their own Self Improvement Club. (Courtesy of the Black Heritage Society of Washington State.)

The Red Cross made masks for people to wear during the influenza epidemic of 1918. These employees of Seattle's Stewart & Holmes Drug Company comply. Photo by Max Loudon. (Courtesy of Special Collections Div., Univ. of Washington Libraries, Neg. #1538.

Volunteers at the Spokane Canteen pose before one of the many troop trains that they served. 1918. (Courtesy of the Eastern
Washington State Historical Society, Spokane)

Daughters of U.S. War Veterans formed the Fortson-Thygesen Drum and Bugle Corps, named after two Seattle officers who gave their lives for their country. 1933. (Courtesy of the Everett Public Library).

Members of the Junior League of Tacoma get help from husbands and boyfriends to produce the fabulous "Follies." 1947. (Courtesy of the Junior League of Tacoma)

Following the Armistice, much of the work continued, but at a less frenetic pace. Volunteers aided returning veterans and their families in many ways. There was a revitalization of programs that had lapsed during the war, including lifesaving, water safety, first aid, and home nursing classes.

As the Great Depression of the 1930s deepened, local Red Cross societies worked with the Washington Federation of Women's Clubs and government extension agents to teach nutrition and to encourage preservation of food surpluses. Presaging the "victory gardens" of World War II, the Red Cross gave away packages of garden seeds, urging homemakers to grow their own fruits and vegetables.

In more recent times, the Red Cross has kept apace with the changing world, adjusting its programs to societal needs. It has continued to promote public health, safety, and education and to provide disaster assistance in both war and peace time.

The Junior League

Turn-of-the-century social reform movements prompted a group of affluent young women in New York City to want to help less fortunate slum dwellers of the lower East Side. This was the beginning of the Junior Leagues

which from the start realized that effective voluntary service required training and education programs. As the original members married and moved to other parts of the country, they founded new leagues. A prerequisite was a group of young women who had already demonstrated a commitment to community service.

Tacoma's Ruth Anderson Wheeler and her husband had inherited the region's first brick and tile business on land rich in clay near Eatonville. On occasional visits to the cookhouse, Mrs. Wheeler said, "I got interested in the children up there. I was always having a group of two or three children down to have their tonsils out. Their parents were Czecks. They didn't understand English and didn't come with the children. I thought more should be done. When I built my home, I invited about eight friends." The young women met regularly at the Wheeler home for two or three years, bringing with them some of Tacoma's first portable sewing machines on which they stitched garments for Clay City children.

Like Wheeler, several of her friends had attended Annie Wright Academy, followed by high school and sometimes college at Bryn Maur, Wellesley, or other Eastern girls' schools. Joining them were newcomers with similar backgrounds. By 1921, the group, which had grown to 26, sought a more permanent identity and a structure that would enable it to better serve their community.

The members organized as the Tacoma Junior Charity League—later renamed Junior League of Tacoma (JLT)—and elected Lucille Davis, who had previously been a member of the Cranford League, as president. Tacoma was just in time to become one of 30 charter members of the Association of Junior Leagues of America, joining Portland and San Francisco as the only chapters on the west coast. Sister leagues soon followed in Seattle and Spokane and later in Yakima. One of JLT's founders, Helen Bailey Murray, traveled for weeks at a time to fulfill her obligations as an early member of the national board.

At first, JLT members continued to sew, choosing the Children's Home—the favorite charity of several of their mothers and grandmothers—as the recipient of their handiwork. Another early project was the Motor Squad to assist the Red Cross with post-war transport services, particularly for Visiting Nurses. League member Eugenia Hufford Currie, who had begun driving for the Red Cross at age 14, was well equipped to advise new volunteers.

The seriousness of the founding members' commitment is evident in President Wheeler's 1922 annual report. "We feel sure that . . . [the] members will continue to take their part ably and usefully in the life of this

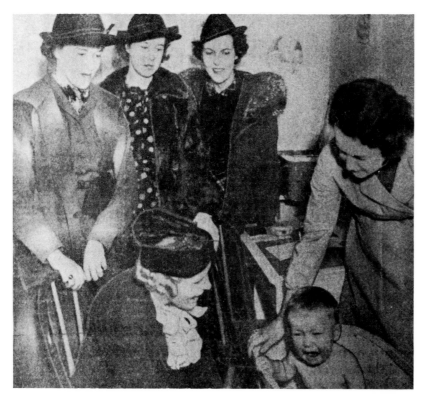

The Well-Baby Clinic at the Pierce County Hospital was the Junior League of Tacoma's major project in the 1920s and 1930s. Here, new provisional members watch Junior Leaguer, Elvira Griggs, as she weighs an unhappy visitor. The league's thrift shop supported the clinic. Photo by Turner Richards, published in the *Tacoma News Tribune*, October 9, 1937 (Courtesy of the *Tacoma News Tribune*)

and a milk fund, patronage of arts programs including children's theater, and founding of the Occupational Therapy Workshop at Tacoma General Hospital. (The latter was the beginning of the city's Crippled Children's School, now a vital part of the Tacoma Public Schools). Leagues in Spokane and Seattle began with a similar array of projects.

By the 1930s, Washington's leagues had established courses for newly elected "provisionals" who became full-fledged members only on successful completion of their training year. At age 40 or 45, they would leave active status to become "sustainers."

An important part of the Junior League's program has always been fundraising as a means of endowing its community service projects. In the early years, there were style shows, charity balls, teas, and rummage sales (precursors of the later more permanent thrift shops). For the fabulous "Follies," local leagues leased costumes and hired producers from New York to rehearse members in song and dance routines which they performed to S.R.O. audiences at their cities' finest theaters.

The Tacoma league sponsored a wide range of programs including a lecture by Will Durant and an exhibition boxing match featuring Jack Dempsey; the Spokane league sponsored performances by actress Cornelia Otis Skinner and by the Alvera Street Marionettes. During the 1930s, the Seattle league began publication of its award-winning *Puget Soundings* magazine.

Through the years, the Junior Leagues have kept apace with a changing world. In the 1960s, the one-time bastion of society ladies began to accept working women as members, accommodating their schedules with evening provisional classes. Today's membership is open to any young woman who wants to make a serious commitment to voluntarism.

The Spokane, Tacoma, Seattle and Yakima leagues have contributed to their communities' vitality with projects to enhance city libraries, parks, art and historical museums, the public schools and children's theater. They have cooperated with other agencies by establishing a variety of programs to counter child abuse, assist victims of domestic violence, promote literacy, advocate for the rights of handicapped people, and more.

At the heart of their mission is the training of effective volunteers who work in partnership with the communities they serve. Washington's leagues participate actively in the association of more than 260 Junior Leagues from the United States, Canada and Mexico which has become a powerful voice for social change.

community by never giving any but efficient service, as not just their pride is at stake, but the pride of the Tacoma Junior League and one failure to answer for promised service does more harm to its name . . . than a year's earnest work will be remembered."

By 1922, the JLT was providing volunteers for the YWCA, the Girl Scouts, St. Joseph's Hospital, the city's Federation of Social Agencies, the City Hall Clinic, the Public Health Nursing Association and the Community Chest. Among its early major projects were the endowment of a maternity bed in local hospitals, the establishment of "well-baby clinics"

The Tacoma Junior League hosted a fundraiser, featuring Jack Dempsey at the Stadium Bowl. Here, President Marjorie Jeffries Shaneman (now Baker) greets him. League member Presley Ellis later noted, "Great pains were taken to have any kind of liquor available to satisfy the fighter's thirst after his bout. The committee recalled its surprise, when he asked for 'a cup of tea, please.'" (Courtesy of Marjorie Jeffries Shaneman Baker)

Camp Fire

In 1921, when Amy Cheney sprained her ankle on a trail near Puget Sound's Three Tree Point, her only companion was her pre-school-aged daughter, now Betty Stadum. Stadum remembers a group of girls dressed in middies who chanced upon the hapless pair and offered to help. The girls borrowed a wheelbarrow and toted her mother home, where they proceeded to tape up the injured ankle. When Cheney asked what she could do to thank them, the girls—who by good fortune had just completed their first-aid training—asked her to become a Camp Fire guardian. The mishap ushered in a lifetime of Camp Fire for Stadum who joined a Firefly group at age seven and is still an enthusiastic volunteer.

Locally, groups of Camp Fire Girls began to organize in the early teens. Their inspiration was a magazine article that told about the new American association for girls, age seven to eighteen, which was founded in 1910 to "perpetuate the spiritual ideals of the home" and to develop health and character. From the beginning local Camp Fire Girls made their own ceremonial gowns, beads and the leather badges that they earned for community service and for outdoor survival accomplishments, such as frying an egg on a rock, or swimming a mile.

In Seattle the different groups began to band together in 1919 under the leadership of Ruth Brown who helped them to acquire and develop a campsite. The following year, thanks to generous donations from members of the Kiwanis, the organization owned its permanent Camp Sealth with a mile and a half of beach front on Vashon Island. In addition to outdoor skills and crafts, the campers learned to work with groups. The girls contributed to operational costs with doughnut sales (a precursor of the Camp Fire mint).

One of the goals of Camp Fire is for young people to get to know their community and to become involved. To this end, the Seattle organization had paid staff and a board that orchestrated a variety of city-wide and regional activities. In 1923, a generous benefactor gave the organization the "Camaraderie," a World War I, wooden-hulled freighter that, following the Armistice, was never completed. Workers transformed the officers' quarters into residences for paid staff; they converted the large holds into recreational areas; and the crews' quarters served as a dormitory for out-of-town visitors. Until the early 1930s, when it collapsed in a storm, the Camaraderie was a popular community center for the middie-clad girls and their guardians.

Today, there are 18 Camp Fire councils throughout the state, which serve both girls and boys. As in the past the members continue to enjoy summer camp and to earn merit badges for their accomplishments in crafts, leadership and community service.

Girl Scouts

In 1920, Tacoma's Catherine Wilkeson (later Lambert) completed her education at Columbia University, along with intensive training in Girl Scout work at the national headquarters in New York City. She returned to her native Tacoma with official credentials and the title of State Director of Girl Scouts for the State of Washington. Nationally, the organization was founded in 1912 in Savannah, Georgia, by Juliette Gordon Low (who had been a leader of Girl Guide troops in England), to promote good citizenship, sociability and outdoor life among girls, age seven to seventeen.

While scouting was well established in the East, it remained for women like Wilkenson to pioneer the movement in the West. Taking up her new post, she said "I am so eager to get started and have my own troop and captains, so we may work towards a Girl Scout camp, for the nearest camp is in Colorado. Wherever the Girl Scout movement is started, there is a marked decrease of delinquency, and a general toning up of the families of the girls."[4]

From the beginning, troops in Washington state followed the national guidelines set up by Low. Each troop was advised by a captain who had to be at least 21 years old. In Girl Scouts, members won merit badges and promotions in rank for community service, for demonstrated proficiency in 56 different activities, and for being "loyal, honorable, kind, and helpful in the home, in the school, in the field, on the playground, and in the Club Room." Their watchword was "Be prepared!" and their slogan was "Do a good turn daily."

In her home town, Wilkeson started the state's first organized troop at Lowell School with a membership of 16 girls. Prior to this time, girls and mothers, who had experienced scouting in other states, had tried to start a few lone troops, but did not have access to the uniforms, merit badges, camps or national training programs. Working without remuneration, Wilkeson energetically set forth to organize other troops in Seattle, Bellingham, Foster, Renton, Anacortes, Concrete, National, Chehalis, South Bend, PeEll, Pullman, and Winthrop—all within 14 months. She then accepted an even greater challenge, as the first Regional Director for the Northwest States.

Christening the "Camaraderie." (Courtesy of Camp Fire of Seattle/King County)

From the early days, Camp Fire extended itself regionally. There were Western and Eastern Washington Conferences which met annually, frequently with a national executive as an honored guest. There were exchange camperships with girls from western Washington going to camp near Spokane on Lake Coeur d'Alene or to the Yakima area in the mountains, and with girls from eastern Washington attending Camp Sealth.

By the late teens, there were Girl Scout troops in Seattle, started by girls and their mothers who had come to the city from other parts of the United States and who wanted to continue the program. Here members of the Fir Tree Girl Scout Troop, number one, pose for their photo, which appeared in the 1922 Lincoln High School Annual. (Courtesy of the Seattle Public Schools Archives)

An outward symbol of the Girl Scout's commitment was the uniform, designed by Juliette Low. It was a one-piece khaki-colored dress with a black tie, topped off by a wide-brimmed hat. Merit badges were proudly displayed on the long sleeves. With military precision, the organization took seriously its uniform, as illustrated by this notice in a 1922 issue of the *Tacoma Tribune:* "It is not proper for Girl Scouts to appear on the streets in knickerbockers, bloomers, or any other non-regulation uniform."[5]

By 1923, courses were being given for Girl Scout directors at state normal schools in Bellingham and Ellensburg. The next year, the Lions Club and the American Legion gave their assistance to the Tacoma Girl Scouts to purchase a 22-acre campsite on Horsehead Bay, which replaced the leased camp that the organization had previously used. Hundreds of girls attended this and other camps at a cost of $6.00 per week.

Among their activities, the Girl Scouts and the younger Brownies helped needy families, took May baskets to hospital patients, and collected clothing to send to destitute orphans in Europe. There were visits from national leaders, leadership training camps, and regional rallies, such as the 1927 pageant for international peace that attracted 500 members to Tacoma's Stadium Bowl. In the same year, eight Girl Scouts—among them the state's future governor Dixy Lee Ray—climbed to the summit of Mt. Rainier, while Norma Judd (now Raver)—a member of Tacoma's first Girl Scout troup—attended the World Camp in Geneva, Switzerland.

Through the years, membership has ballooned, forcing changes in structure and revisions to keep apace with the needs of girls from five to eighteen years of age. Today five councils serve the State of Washington. The original Tacoma troop is part of the Pacific Peaks Girl Scout Council, headquartered in Tumwater, which has a membership of 619 troops with more than 7,000 registered girls and 2,000 adult volunteers.

Norma Judd Raver, who still remains involved, notes that between 1921 and 1988, dues have increased from 25¢ to $4.00 per year and the uniform has changed. She says, "Two of the most exciting recent developments throughout the state have been a program for five-year-olds, known as 'Daisy Scouts' and the exploration of careers by Senior Girl Scouts through long-term volunteer service under the supervision of a professional in the chosen field." Among its priorities, the organization takes handicapped girls into the mainstream, including camp activities. Raver says "The Girl Scout program is geared to help the growing girl learn to face challenges and become a resourceful and responsible citizen."

Home demonstration agents were and are an important part of Extension work. Their subjects range from textiles, to nutrition, to stretching the budget, to family living. County agents trained local leaders to work with women and girls in rural communities. This woman shows how to make a flaky pie crust. Photo by Asahel Curtis. (Courtesy of the Washington State Historical Society, Tacoma, Photo #42442)

4-H and Home Extension Clubs

World War I galvanized the commitment on the part of clubwomen, the Red Cross and government to conservation. Nowhere was the mission taken more seriously than in rural areas, where food supplies were produced. An important part of the effort was the 4-H program, which took root and branched out into rural life. The motto, "Head, Heart, Health and Hands" depicts ethics, ingrained in farming communities, where families rely on their own resourcefulness, and where "neighbor helping neighbor" is an unspoken rule. Boys joined 4-H agricultural clubs, while girls participated in home economics clubs.

The youth program was part of the federally funded Extension Service which was managed by Washington State College in cooperation with the U.S. Department of Agriculture and county governments. During the war, the thrust was primarily economic, emphasizing production and conservation of food. "Demonstration trains" criss-crossed the state, stopping in rural communities, where men, women, boys and girls turned out for instruction in agriculture and home economics.

There were estimates that the 4-H program could mean the addition of $150,000 worth of food supplies to the state. At first, public schools and teachers were involved in the local leadership, along with volunteers. According to veteran Extension worker, Russell Turner, "Some of the state leaders thought 4-H leaders should be paid; others thought it should be on a voluntary basis. The latter group prevailed, and the shift gradually was made away from having most of the 4-H leaders drawn from the school teaching ranks."[6] Rural high schools later sponsored the Future Homemakers of America and the Future Farmers of America—extracurricular clubs for students.

Through their 4-H clubs, girls at first contributed to the war effort. They planted "victory gardens," canned and preserved produce, and like their mothers, spent their free time knitting washcloths and socks. In the post-war period, the clubs helped girls to hone their homemaking skills. Members entered their handiwork in competitions at local, state and interstate fairs. They also attended county camp and state 4-H camp at WSC in Pullman, where hundreds of members took over the campus, living in the dormitories, fraternizing with friends, and taking classes in Home Economics and Agriculture.

Like their daughters, women joined garden and home extension clubs. They kept abreast of issues, especially those related to rural areas, learned

The Thurston County Canning Club won prizes at the Washington State Fair in 1917. Early 4-H'ers often wore uniforms like these, emblazoned with their 4-leaf-clover emblem. (From Washington State University, Extension Miscellaneous Publication 55, 1961)

about the latest homemaking technology and techniques, and entered their creations in adult categories at the fairs. An example of an especially active organization was the Lewis County Council of Homemakers which in 1924 had more than 1,000 members from 40 different clubs. From her office in Chehalis, Grace Enzleson, the county's extension agent from WSC, offered supervision and support to the clubs, each of which served a community with a population of less than 2,000. Three times a year, the members converged in Chehalis for well-attended meetings with instruction in textiles, food preservation and home management.

During the Great Depression, which engulfed rural Washington during the early 1920s, the women's and girls' clubs again turned their attention to conservation, contributing what they could to help. When trainloads of cotton bales arrived in the state from Texas, girls and their mothers gathered in Grange halls to make cotton mattresses. At the time, they were a welcome change for many whose beds were sheets of cardboard.

More recently, girls have joined boys in clubs devoted to raising livestock. With help from their leaders, they carefully monitor the growth of their calf, lamb, or piglet with hopes of making it a champion at the county fair. In addition to the prestige, a prize-winning animal can be lucrative, helping the young person to pay for college or to save for the future.

The Extension Homemakers Clubs and 4-H were a needed stimulus that gave farm women and children some of the networking structures and community pride, enjoyed by their urban counterparts. Along with community schools, the Grange and other organizations, they enriched farm life and helped to stem the flight of young people to cities.

Today, Washington State University's Cooperative Extension Service has agents in every county in the state. They continue to provide leadership training for volunteers who in turn lead 4-H and Homemakers' clubs. In addition to members' individual projects, today's 4-H clubs emphasize community service projects that range from picking up roadside trash to building flower planters for downtown streets. As in the past, Home Extension responds to people's needs. In depressed rural areas and in cities, agents provide information on such topics as stretching family budgets and low-cost, nutritious food preparation.

Notes

1. Seattle/King County Chapter of the American National Red Cross, Annual Report, 1941–2.
2. Patricia S. Goetter, *A History of the Inland Empire Chapter of the American Red Cross, 1881–1981* (Spokane, 1981), unpub. p. 8.
3. Excerpt from LeEtta Sanders King's Oral History Transcript, BL-KNG-75-5em. May 16 and 25, 1975. Washington State Oral/Aural History Program (174–75).
4. Emma Otis, *Historical Record of Girl Scouting in Pierce County,* (Tacoma, 1962), unpub., p. 7.
5. ibid., p. 10.
6. Russell M. Turner, *The First 45 Years: a History of Cooperative Extension in Washington State,* (Pullman, 1961) p. 9.

Woman feeding hens on Skookumchulk Ranch near Yakima. Long before World War I, rural women had sold their butter, eggs, homegrown produce and preserves to contribute to their family income. Since 1889, rural women had joined the Grange where they participated with men in social, economic, and political life. (Courtesy of the Washington State Historical Society. Asahel Curtis #21072)

A one-room schoolhouse in rural King County. Photo by Asahel Curtis. (Courtesy of the Seattle Public Schools Archives)

Education

6

At the heart of early Washington women's activities was their commitment to education. As witnessed in other chapters, women's groups established arts institutes, nursing schools, Americanization programs for newly arrived immigrants and more. In children's hospitals, orphanages, girls' detention centers and homes for unwed mothers, women volunteered as teachers and counselors.

The settlement of the Pacific Northwest coincided with events in the East that opened up unprecedented opportunities for women. A major tenet of post-revolutionary Republican idealism was that women should serve as models for their children, educating them to become good citizens. Consequently, girls' seminaries blossomed throughout New England and New York, while established academies also began to admit female students. As women gained academic training, many chose to enter the acceptable field of education. Missionary wives, Catholic nuns and single women teachers braved the westward journey to Washington because they were determined to teach children the three Rs and to instill in them Christian values and good citizenship.

Wives of Protestant missionaries held their first classes in their own homes. At Waiilatpu (near Walla Walla), Narcissa Whitman taught Cayuse children and the 12 orphans that she and her husband had adopted. At Tshimikain (near Kettle Falls), Mary Richardson Walker fashioned her own slates so that she could instruct native American children along with her own. Similarly, mothers on isolated homesteads continued to organize neighborhood schools well into the twentieth century. Mother Joseph and the Sisters of Providence built academies in Vancouver, Yakima, Olympia, Colfax, Sprague, Walla Walla, and Moxee, opening their doors to all children regardless of race, parentage, or creed.

Indian Schools

As Indian tribes signed treaties and moved to reservations, Protestant missionaries and Catholics alike cooperated with the government to establish boarding schools. Prior to this, several Native Americans throughout the territory had already befriended early Catholic and Protestant missionaries and had converted to Christianity. However, in so doing, they had not abandoned the teachings of their tribal Elders which were their history and which served as guidelines for living in this world.

Lucy Abigail Peet Cowley and her husband, the Rev. Thomas Henry Cowley, were missionaries at Lapwai on the Nez Perce Reservation, before they moved to Spokane at the invitation of local Native Americans. Like other missionary wives, Mrs. Cowley taught her own and Indian children. (Courtesy of Margaret Paine Cowles)

Boarding Schools

The boarding school sought to negate what for many was a workable transition. Teachers were mandated to "civilize and Christianize" Indian children—in other words to do their utmost to obliterate ancient cultural and spiritual traditions and to transform Native Americans into images of

Swinomish Indian school. (Courtesy of the Skagit County Historical Museum).

white people. Sometimes, teachers realized that the negative approach was ill-conceived and worked with Indian families to make the best of the situation and build mutual respect. In so doing, they risked losing their jobs.

More often, teachers, many of whom were single Protestant women and Catholic nuns, set forth with zeal to accomplish their mission. In militaristic boarding schools, they forced children to speak English, while teaching them that the ways of their elders were pagan and backward. Indian children were punished for speaking their native tongue. Ella Aquino, who attended school on the Lummi Reservation, could never forget the horrible humiliation when, if children were caught playing hookey, the police arrested their parents and escorted them to the jail on the school grounds to serve a month-long sentence. Amelia Sohappy, who was shipped off to boarding school in Oregon, refused an order to become either Protestant or Catholic and recalls sneaking off with friends to speak Yakima. When the harsh rules eventually gave way, she became caretaker of her tribe's longhouse.

Indian parents sometimes resisted the mandate to take away their children and tried to keep them out of school. Others recognized schooling as a necessity to enable younger generations to adapt to a changing world. Confident that the strength of the family and the tribe would prevail, one Makah father said, "the only thing we can do is learn to be better than the white people."[1]

Clubwomen's Involvement

Social reform movements and wartime emergencies, when Indians served in the military and in defense-related industries, led to gradual liberalization and an eventual end to the strict federal mandate. In the 1920s, the Washington State Federation of Women's Clubs became concerned about the high rate of illiteracy and illness among the state's 80 to 90 tribes, numbering 8,141 individuals. They noted that Indians were in many cases suspicious of whites and that the government's Indian Bureau was providing woefully inadequate medical care. At the time, the government was planning to grant Indians citizenship.

The WSFWC created an Indian Welfare Department to see that education, vocational training and medical care were available to Indians. On seven of the state's reservations, clubwomen organized classes in such activities as sewing, balanced meal planning, canning, and first aid, along with Boy and Girl Scout troops and 4-H clubs. In addition to practical skills, Native American women learned to conduct meetings using the rules of parliamentary procedure. Some of them organized their own clubs and joined the federation.

Indian culture became a highlight of WSFWC conventions, as clubwomen set forth to collect Indian art, essays by Indians, and stories to document their heritage. At the Longview convention in the 1930s, Sally Sicade Navarre of the Puyallup tribe became state chairman of the music division and presented a program on American Indian music. Nationally, clubwomen were engaged in similar activities, but for the most part to a lesser degree than in Washington State, where the history of settlement was still young and where clubwomen were aware of the rapidity with which the history of fragmented tribes was slipping away, unrecorded.

Native American Women's Leadership

The Civil Rights Movement of the 1960s and 1970s heralded acts of Congress to restore Indian rights, including the Indian Self-Determination and Education Act, the Indian Religious Freedom Act, and the Indian Community College Assistance Act. In Washington State, Native Amer-

Group of Colville Indian girls in long dresses, who could have been attending boarding school. n.d. (Courtesy of the Eastern Washington State Historical Society, Spokane)

ican women founded service and advocacy organizations, including the American Indian Women's Service League and the Northwest Indian Women's Circle. In addition, they have played leadership roles in such organizations as the United Indians of all Tribes. Among their activities, these organizations have helped create educational programs to restore Indian culture and history to school curricula. In addition, several Washington colleges and universities now offer courses taught by Native Americans on Indian heritage and issues.

Vi Hilbert, an Upper Skagit Salish Elder, was deeply concerned that the heritage of her people was being lost and decided to devote herself to its preservation. A highly acclaimed folk artist and storyteller, she taught Native American language and literature at the University of Washington for 20 years, until her recent retirement. She has translated and published Salish stories, along with a dictionary of the Lushootseed language. As a participant in a video, "The Elders Have a Way of Teaching," she was one of eight Salish Elders who told stories about the mythological origins of familiar geographic landmarks, while passing on philosophical teachings to younger generations about how to live in the world.[2]

Ella Aquino, who moved from the Lummi reservation to Seattle in the 1950s, helped found the American Indian Services League, a support group for the city's Indians. Once when someone asked her why she did so many things for others, she answered: "Somebody's got to do it. I've got to show our young people that if a little old lady with an eighth-grade education can manage it, they can. This community is my family and I love them all." In her late 70s, Aquino earned her high school equivalency diploma.[3]

In Eatonville, the Nisqually Tribe and the DOVE (Development of the Ohop Valley for Education) Center, founded by Meryl Pruitt, have cooperated in the development of the Pioneer Farm Museum and a traveling, hands-on museum that tours to schools throughout the state. Focusing on daily life, the museum demonstrates Native American and pioneer techniques for grinding grains, sharpening tools, churning butter, carding wool, etc. Children try on pioneer and Native American clothing, while learning how Norwegian settlers and the Nisqually lived, side by side, in the Ohop Valley.

Public Schools

As settlements developed throughout the Washington Territory, one of the primary thrusts was the community school. It symbolized stature and stability with a commitment to the future and usually predated hospitals, sidewalks, city halls or other public accommodations. Most of the early settlers in Washington had had some education themselves and naturally desired the same for their children. For the most part, they had attended public schools, which they preferred to a parochial education.

Rena Cooness was related to George and Mary Jane Washington, black founders of Centralia. She poses on the beach with other Centralia teachers. (Washington Women's Heritage Project Records, University of Washington Libraries)

Pioneer Schools

For fledgling communities, the single schoolmarm was a godsend. Unencumbered by spouse or family, she would work long hours for considerably less than a man. In dimly-lit "shack" schools, she swept the floor, carried wood and water, built the fire, and taught grades one through eight with pupils ranging from age five to as old as 25. As part of her meager pay, she received living expenses which often meant "boarding out"—lodging with different families and sharing their daughters' beds.

In 1890, a Newcastle teacher, Lydia Dwyer, wrote letters to her fiancé about having to cope with 66 children, grades one to four. She also had to cope with the fifth to eighth grade teacher whose "degrading amusements" often kept him away from the classroom. Whenever he was absent, she was responsible for his students as well as her own.[4]

Women Administrators

In 1870, Seattle citizens built their first public school and hired Elizabeth Ordway as the faculty. When 125 pupils showed up on the first day of class, she sent the youngest ones home "to ripen a little" until additional teachers could be hired. An ardent suffragist, her career waxed political and in 1881, she was elected Kitsap County's Superintendent of Schools.

By the 1890s, women had gained a strong presence in school administration, especially as elementary school principals. Clara McCarty Wilts, the first graduate of the University of Washington, taught school in Sumner and Tacoma before superintending Pierce County's schools. Thurston County's school superintendent, Pamela Case Hale, was a founding member of the Olympia Women's Club and also of the State Teachers' Association in 1889.

In Walla Walla, Josephine Corliss Preston headed the county's schools until 1912 when Washington voters (including newly enfranchised women) elected her as state superintendent. She was actively involved in the State Federation of Women's Clubs and in other women's and professional associations which proved to be a strong base of support for her programs.

Rural Schools and Community Centers

One of her major concerns was the sad state of rural education and the welfare of the rural teacher for whom "boarding out" often became intolerable. Enlisting the support of women's clubs, Preston promoted teachers' cottages which were built near schools, especially in rural areas. With the privacy of a "teacherage" to call home after a hard day's work, rural teachers were soon sticking with their jobs.

While in Walla Walla, Preston had induced a farm couple to send their son to school in town. When he went astray in the saloons, the family held her to blame. She realized that rural boys and girls needed to be educated in the country where they could live at home with their families. Women's clubs throughout the state rallied to support her idea of the "community center" which doubled as the country school. Since the school building was public property, it made sense to use it to the fullest. After school hours, the centers drew widely scattered neighbors together for meetings, recreation, and bonding as a community.

So successful were Preston's "teacherages" and "community centers," that with the help of the General Federation of Women's Clubs, the systems rapidly swept rural America. Preston, who was also president of the National Education Association, gave women's organizations direction both locally and nationally, helping them to increase their effectiveness in the support of the schools. In Washington State, her club sisters gave strong support to several other innovations that took shape during her 16-year administration, including kindergartens, hot lunches, and school bus transportation. In 1923, Washington's public schools received a number one rating from the U.S. Bureau of Education.

Growth and Development

In 1928, when Preston left office, the Island and Snohomish County district elected school principal, Pearl A. Wanamaker, to the House of Representatives. As a legislator, she made the schools her major concern and is credited directly with several improvements in the state's educational programs, among them 875 new school buildings, an increase in teachers' minimum wage from $500 to $2,780, and passage of the Showalter Bill which provided basic state support of 25¢ per day for each pupil.

Journalist Marci Whitney says: "With an indomitable spirit she politicked in Olympia like they had never seen before. Penny-pinching legislators reluctant to go along with her school budgets would groan, 'She drives right into your hometown and tells your constituents you're voting against their kids.' "[5] Wanamaker resigned from the legislature in 1940, so that she, like Preston, could serve a 16-year-term as State Superintendent of Public Instruction. Always the champion of children's issues, she had the strong backing of club women.

Children and teachers pose in front of Seattle's first Central School in May, 1883. Photo by Asahel Curtis. (Courtesy of Special Collections Div., University of Washington Libraries, A. Curtis Photo #62985)

Graduating class from the Ellensburg Normal School in 1893. The state normal schools were in Ellensburg, Bellingham and Cheney where students could originally earn a teaching certificate within two years. The schools later became four-year colleges and then universities. As in this photograph, most of the early graduates were single women who prepared to teach in local schools. (Courtesy of Central Washington University)

Lizzie Ordway was one of the women lured West by Asa Mercer's promises of jobs and bachelors. While the other "Mercer Girls" eventually married, Ordway held off her suitors declaring, "Nothing could induce me to relinquish the life of single blessedness." After years of teaching, she became Kitsap County's Superintendent of Schools. She was also a devoted suffragist. (Courtesy of the Seattle Public Schools Archives)

Special Education

One of Wanamaker's legacies was the movement to integrate physically handicapped and developmentally limited children, whenever possible, into the regular classroom. Her program had antecedents in the Seattle Public Schools, where in 1910, Nellie A. Goodhue had pioneered the Child Study Laboratory, the forerunner of the later guidance department and special education programs. Working in cooperation with the University of Washington, Goodhue and her staff interviewed and tested up to 4,000 pupils per year, studying each individual's problems and helping the child, its parents and teachers to understand each other.

Under Goodhue's tutelage, the school district's Cascade Special School developed individualized instruction programs. Children with severe limitations were still sent to Medical Lake. However, many others were able to remain in the public schools. For some, the special classes treated reading disabilities or other handicaps, enabling the child to adjust to a normal classroom. Others who remained in the special school had an unprecedented opportunity to achieve their potential.

Martha Knox Dorman (seated, right) and her husband, Hiner, pioneered on a farm near Ritzville. With her are her daughters, Lois Woehr and Alice Chargois (standing) and Louie Dorman (seated). With the exception of Lois, all lived on the farm, then owned by Alice and her husband, Victor. They donated an acre of land to the state for the rural Marcellus School, which became a community center for neighbors. (Courtesy of Mildred Chargois Tanner).

Mildred and Doris Chargois attended the Marcellus School. They later earned lifetime teaching certificates after four years at Washington State College and Cheney Normal School. Both taught in the Seattle elementary schools until the late 1930s, when they married. (At the time, the city's schools did not allow married women to teach.) Doris Hahn later resumed teaching at the Denmark School in Kittitas, while Mildred Tanner taught in Ritzville and Spokane. (Courtesy of Mildred Chargois Tanner)

Nationally, Goodhue's work predated mental health care centers. On her retirement, she said: "I can conceive of no greater thrill, no greater compensation for my years spent in teaching, than to know I have lightened the burdens of little children. Every child has been a new problem—a new individual with distinct needs and peculiarities and, because I have treated them just as I would grown-ups in trouble, there are men and women all over the United States who are now happy because I helped carry their burdens when they were children."[6]

"PTA"

Shortly after the turn-of-the-century, support for public schools gained momentum with the concurrent developments of the child psychology movement and the founding of Mothers' Congresses and Parent-Teacher Associations. Mothers, who had traditionally raised their children by instinct, began to form circles to discuss emerging scientific studies of child development, both mental and physical. Working with teachers, they hoped to create better opportunities for their children.

Abby Williams Hill on the front page of the *Los Angeles Examiner.* She was a featured speaker at the convention of the National Congress of Mothers. (*Los Angeles Examiner,* May 14, 1907)

In 1905, Tacoma's Abby Williams Hill attended one of the early meetings of the national Mothers' Congress in Washington, D.C. where she accepted the appointment of organizer for the state of Washington. She returned home to drum up support, starting with the larger school districts and fueling a movement that quickly swept the state. Hill and her supporters set forth with determination to draw every mother and teacher in Washington into a study circle.

In 1911, representatives from all over the state came to Tacoma for the first meeting of the Washington Congress of Mothers and Parent-Teacher Association. Mothers' clubs sponsored a variety of fundraising events, using proceeds for underprivileged children and for such amenities as playground equipment, landscaping, or musical instruments for their schools. With the cooperation of the garden clubs, they launched a popular school garden movement where pupils planted and tended their own plots. Their three-fold purpose was to give the children wholesome exercise, to teach them the rudiments of horticulture, and to beautify their communities.

In an advocacy role, they supported women's suffrage, clean government, and prohibition. They also voiced their opinions regarding such school-related issues as student dress codes, sex-segregated programs, blueprint designs for new schools, and playground safety.

In 1914, Nell Hoyt, mother of a young child in Tacoma, organized the first "pre-school circle," which became part of the state's Mothers' Congress. Five years later, the National Congress adopted the Washington Congress' guidelines for pre-school units and named Hoyt as director of the new department.

Hoyt and some of her friends had questioned the prevailing hypothesis that problems of children under school age were purely physical. They maintained that children began to grow mentally and spiritually in early childhood. The clubs met in homes and included parents, grandparents, nurses, kindergarten leaders and professionals interested in small children. In 1920, Hoyt noted that the word "pre-school" (later preschool) which she had coined was used freely by the general public.

During its history PTAs have helped pass child-labor and school attendance laws, establish juvenile courts, school-lunch programs, kindergartens, libraries and vocational education. By the 1950s, PTA had acquired a middle-class image of white-gloved women, sipping coffee, nibbling cookies and planning their next bake sale. Membership fell off until the 1980s, when elementary school enrollment ballooned with the latest wave of Baby Boomers.

Members of Seattle's Oak Lake Mothers Club pose in a whimsical airplane cutout at the Congress of Mothers Convention, held in Tacoma in May, 1912. From left to right are: Mrs. McMillan, Pres.; Mrs. Norris, Sec.; Mrs. Pugh; Mrs. Geo. Miller; and Mrs. M. A. Rothweiler, Delegate. (Courtesy of the Seattle Public Schools Archives).

The result for PTA has been a 41% increase to a current state level of 113,155 members. Contemporary PTAs and Parent-Teacher-Student Associations (PTSAs) attract both mothers and fathers of diverse ethnicity who are eager to improve the quality of their children's education. Among the issues that the association tackles are child abuse, school desegregation, and drug, sex and AIDS education. As in the past, the PTAs often come to the rescue when schools need money for special programs or events.

Private Schools

In the 1880s, moneyed Washingtonians, having no local choice for quality education, commonly sent their daughters to Eastern boarding schools. Some were therefore overjoyed with the territory's first private academies, finding comfort in the fact that good academic training in a Christian environment was no longer 3,000 miles away.

The private parochial schools with their imposing buildings and exemplary academic and cultural programs prompted newly organized women's clubs and labor unions to launch a campaign for quality education in the public schools. As curricula and facilities improved, most Washington citizens confidently enrolled their children in the schools that their tax dollars supported. Unlike older tradition-bound parts of the country, the Pacific Northwest today has few private academies or elite girls' schools.

Holy Names

In 1880, the Sisters of the Holy Names of Jesus and Mary journeyed from Portland to Seattle, bringing with them a piano and a mission to establish an academy for girls. According to their leader, Sister Superior Francis Xavier, the piano was symbolic of their devotion to music, which from the beginning was one of their most important subjects. The program was open to girls, regardless of race, creed, or social status.

From humble beginnings in a leaky, rat-infested building, the nuns quickly attracted students and gained a reputation for providing a high quality liberal arts education. The convent school grew so quickly that within three years it was able to build what the local press dubbed the handsomest structure in the Washington Territory. Holy Names Academy gradually extended its programs to include kindergarten through eighth grade and a normal school for teacher training. Some of the sisters went to Spokane to establish Holy Names College, a four-year liberal arts college for women.

Seattle's second Holy Names Academy, constructed in 1908 on Capitol Hill. Photo by Asahel Curtis. (Courtesy of Special Collections Div., University of Washington Libraries. A. Curtis Photo #11255)

In 1908, when Seattle's ambitious project to regrade the city's hills forced the nuns to abandon their original school, they constructed a stately Romanesque building that has since housed their academic programs and served the city. The Spokane sisters closed their college in the 1960s when they moved to the city's former military post to conduct the liberal arts curriculum at the new Fort Wright College. Although that college also eventually closed, the sisters continue to manage the historic fort grounds. In the tradition of their forebears, they are committed to programs in education and the arts.

Annie Wright

Like the Roman Catholic nuns, Episcopalians came west determined to provide a proper education for young ladies. At Walla Walla's St. Paul's School for girls, parents paid tuition in gold, six mule teams of flour, or cattle selected by the head master himself. Henrietta Garretson Wells was the first head mistress of Tacoma's Annie Wright Academy, which opened in 1884. (Her husband, the Rev. Lemuel Wells, later became Bishop of Spokane.) The imposing, American Gothic building accommodated 77 girls—day students and boarders from several states.

Henrietta Garretson Wells, ca. 1884. She was principal of St. Paul's School for Girls in Walla Walla before assuming the same position at Annie Wright Seminary. Later, when her husband was transferred to Spokane, she became principal of that city's Brunot Hall, another exclusive girls' school founded by Episcopalians. (Courtesy of Annie Wright School)

The school had been the dream of the Rt. Rev. John A. Paddock, newly appointed Bishop of the Territory, who saw a need for a facility that could provide academic excellence in a Christian environment. As president of the Northern Pacific Railroad, Charles B. Wright had recently brought the line to its Northwest terminus in Tacoma, thereby linking the region with the East. Sharing Paddock's dream, he became the school's major benefactor, naming it after his daughter Annie.

As part of their education, students were encouraged to take an interest in the community, to assume leadership roles, and to become creative and responsible members of society. Because of the school's high standards, its graduates could enroll in several of the nation's leading women's colleges without entrance examinations.

The first Annie Wright Seminary, built in 1884. (Courtesy of Annie Wright School)

In the 1920s, Annie Wright Seminary, now the Annie Wright School, outgrew its original building and moved to the stately Tudor facilities that overlook Commencement Bay. While the school draws students from all over the world, its greatest impact has been on Tacoma. After college, many Annie Wright alumnae have returned home to Tacoma where they have had a decisive influence on the city's social and cultural development. In turn, they have steadfastly supported their alma mater, contributing financially and in other ways, and often creating a family tradition by enrolling their daughters and granddaughters.

American Association of University Women

The Association of Collegiate Alumnae (after 1921 known as the American Association of University Women) began in New England when educational opportunities for women were few and openings for trained women even fewer. Frustrated by their circumstances, a group of college graduates banded together to advocate for more equitable standards.

As a girl, Ruth Anderson (now Wheeler) attended the first Annie Wright Seminary. After college in the East, she returned to Tacoma, where she was a founding member of the Junior League. She has remained a loyal "Annie," contributing to the school's support and regaling younger generations with anecdotes about its history. (Courtesy of Ruth Anderson Wheeler)

Locally, the association took root in Seattle in 1904, followed by branches in Spokane and Grays Harbor. Founding members were alumnae from prestigious eastern colleges and universities who brought with them their own criteria for institutional accreditation.

Ruth Karr McKee, third from right, was appointed to the UW board of regents in 1917 and was elected president in 1923. She was the granddaughter of pioneer missionary, Mary Richardson Walker. (Courtesy of Special Collections Div., Univ. of Washington Libraries, UW Neg. #3286)

At the University of Washington, the ACA joined forces with the Washington State Federation of Women's Clubs, the Daughters of the American Revolution, campus women's organizations, and others to promote leadership training, role models, and professional orientation for women students. As a result, Isabella Austin advanced from her status of housemother to the first dean of women.

In 1917, Governor Lister appointed Ruth Karr McKee to the University's board of regents—the first woman to serve in that capacity at any of the state's institutions of higher learning. When she was elected president in 1923, she was the first woman to hold the office at any major American university. A UW graduate, McKee had been actively involved in club work in Hoquiam and Gray's Harbor and was past president of the State Federation of Women's Clubs.

While there were breakthroughs and a few outstanding success stories, inequities prevailed. An example was women faculty members who for years had met in the Home Economics Building. In 1927, they were given a room in the long-established Faculty Men's Club but with the stipulation that the front entrance was for men only. Until the 1950s, female colleagues had to use the side door.

Frances Penrose Owen was elected to the Seattle School Board in the 1940s, where she served for 22 years. She was also a member of the Washington State University Board of Regents for 18 years, during which time she became national president of the Association of Governing Boards of Universities and Colleges. At Whitman College in her native Walla Walla, where her father had been president, she became a member of the Board of Overseers. (Courtesy of the Seattle Public Schools Archives).

Young women students relax on the lawn in front of the UW's Denny Hall. 1898. (Courtesy of Special Collections Div., University of Washington Libraries, UW Negative #2218)

Like the Association of Collegiate Alumnae, several other organizations established scholarship and loan funds to assist promising women students. Among the first were the PEO, an organization dedicated to promoting higher education opportunities for women, and the WSFWC.

Efforts to promote equity in academia were only a part of the ACA's agenda. The organization also sought to utilize the college training of its members for the improvement of educational conditions and standards in society. Under the leadership of Margaretha Sheppard Ferris, the Spokane branch purchased a camp in 1922 to give week-long summer respites to poverty stricken mothers and their children. The camp had a resident house-mother and helpers to cook and care for the children. In addition to rest and relaxation, the camp held informal classes for mothers and teachers and for pre-school mothers.

In the early years, AAUW restricted its membership to graduates of institutions that met its own strict standards. While the UW eventually made the grade in 1915, many of Washington's colleges and universities consistently failed. When AAUW relaxed its criteria in the 1930s, local branches increased their membership, since female graduates of any accredited four-year college were then welcome to join. In addition to its involvement in higher education, the association has continued to conduct programs of interest to members in the areas of international relations, education, and culture.

Alaska-Yukon-Pacific Exposition: Woman's Building

In 1909, Washington State staged an extravaganza, the Alaska-Yukon-Pacific Exposition, held on the University of Washington campus. Every major American fair had had its woman's building and the AYP was no exception. As president of the Washington State Federation of Women's Clubs, Lena Erwin Allen of Spokane presented a proposal to the State Fair Commissioners asking that the legislature fund a Woman's Building which would celebrate women's accomplishments and which would later serve as a center for women students.

During the fair, the two-story, wooden structure housed a student YWCA-sponsored restaurant, a nursery which cared for as many as 300 children a day, a juried exhibit of Washington women's arts, and a large reception area. Among the organizations that held conferences in conjunction with the AYP were the National American Woman Suffrage Association, the National Council of Women, the Washington State Federation of Women's Clubs, the State Teachers, the State Nurses, the Women's Christian Temperance Union, and the Eastern Star.

When the AYP closed in the fall of 1909, the building, as planned, became an activity center for campus women. In this capacity it was home to the office of the dean of women, the campus Women's League, the Tolo Club (a senior honorary society which later affiliated with Mortar Board), the Sacajawea and Athena debating teams, Sororia Society for mature women students, and a restaurant where the student YWCA continued to serve nickel lunches.

Women students and faculty, along with visiting club women, came to the center where they launched an impressive number of programs and activities. Community women recruited student volunteers for work in hospitals and social service agencies. Campus women lobbied for the letter "W" for UW women athletes in basketball, rowing, tennis, hockey, handball, and baseball. There were vocational conferences and orientations for new women students. Campus and community women worked together to devise campaign strategies for suffrage, prohibition, and other women's issues.

After seven fruitful years under one roof, the women lost their facility which was converted to a U.S. Government Experimental Mining Station in preparation for World War I. Finally, in 1981, women students reclaimed their building for its original purpose, renaming it Imogen Cunningham Hall in honor of the noted photographer who graduated from the UW in 1907. Once again, the Washington State Federation of Women's Clubs contributes its support, including books for the center's library.[7]

Women in Communications, Inc.

The Alaska-Yukon-Pacific Exposition brought national and international attention to Washington State, benefiting business and attracting newcomers to the region. As a student in the UW's newly created Department of Journalism (the second in the nation), Georgina MacDougall (Davis) had an idea and knew that the time was right to promote it.

MacDougall was one of seven women students in the department to produce the first women's edition of the college newspaper, the *Pacific Daily Wave*. The purpose was to acquaint students with the activities of campus women at other universities, especially those on the Pacific Coast. In April, 1909, just before the opening of the fair, MacDougall and her friend Helen Ross stayed up all night hatching plans to start an honorary society for women journalists.

A few days later, the seven women on the newspaper's staff appeared on campus wearing violet and green ribbons. They had adopted an official pin which was a reproduction of the matrix of the linotype machine and proclaimed themselves Alpha Chapter of Theta Sigma Phi. Junior and senior women in the journalism department were invited to join the new honorary society if they demonstrated literary talent and if they intended to make journalism their life's work.

Ross, the only founding member who owned a typewriter, began corresponding with other universities which were adding departments of journalism. The idea caught fire and within a short time Georgina MacDougall's vision became reality with Alpha Chapter issuing charters to new chapters of Theta Sigma Phi on other campuses throughout the nation.

The Washington State Women's Building at the Alaska-Yukon-Pacific Exposition, 1909. (Courtesy of Special Collections Div., Univ. of Washington Libraries, UW Negative #1581)

Georgina MacDougall, one of the founding members of Theta Sigma Phi which later became Women in Communications, Inc. (Courtesy of Women in Communications, Inc.)

At a later date the society changed its name to Women in Communications, Inc., emphasizing its revised objective of promoting the advancement of women in all fields of communication. According to Barbara Krohn, currently publisher of the *University of Washington Daily,* WICI's greatest achievement was to establish women professionally in a field not traditionally regarded as "women's work."

Notes

1. "Ella Aquino, Indian leader, dies," *Seattle Post-Intelligencer,* October 4, 1988, p. D. 14.
2. "Documentary Tells Story of Salish," *Northwest Ethnic News,* Oct., 1985.
3. Carolyn Marr, Program Coordinator, *Portrait in Time: Photos of the Makah by Samuel G. Morse, 1896–1903,* (The Makah Cultural and Research Center and the Washington State Historical Society, 1987), p. 16.
4. Richard K. and Lucille McDonald, *The Coals of Newcastle* (Issaquah: 1987).
5. Marci Whitney, *Notable Women* (Tacoma, 1977), p. 52.
6. "Teacher Quits after 22 Years of Work Here," *Seattle Post-Intelligencer,* (Spring, 1929).
7. For further information see: Karen J. Blair, "The Limits of Sisterhood: the Woman's Building in Seattle, 1908–1921," *Frontiers,* VII, No. 1, 1984.

Mothers helped to organize the annual 4th of July picnic, sponsored by Seattle's Nihon Gakko (Japanese School). With "Old Glory" at the head of the table, women and children posed in their summer finery for this photograph. There were similar schools in other Japanese/American communities throughout the state where families came from far and wide to celebrate the holiday. Entertainment included performances of traditional dance and the martial arts, along with foot races and baseball. On Saturdays and in the afternoons, after classes were dismissed from the public schools, these children attended the Nihon Gakko, where they studied Japanese. (Courtesy of Special Collections Div., Univ. of Washington Archives, UW Neg. #413)

After classes at the Japanese school, pupils often went on to their dance class where they studied traditional dance. (See Arts chapter.) Here, Madame Nakatani performs with her students at Seattle's Nippon Kan (Japanese Theatre), accompanied by musicians playing the samisen. (Courtesy of Edward and Elizabeth Burke)

Jennie Wesley (Yakima) doing beadwork. (Courtesy of the Washington State Library, Northwest Collection)

Arts

7

Individually and through their organizations, Washington women have always nurtured the artistic and cultural growth of their communities. In the late 19th century, groups of women in all parts of the state began to meet over china teacups for literary readings and musical performances by members. Through the State Federation of Women's Clubs, members promoted the arts in the schools and for the public. Ethnic women from multiple cultural traditions have preserved their dances, music, arts and crafts by celebrating them and teaching them to younger generations. In music, theater, dance, and the visual arts, Washington women have played a catalytic role as artists, teachers, critics and patrons.

Traditional Arts and Crafts

Among the Northwest's first recognized artists were coastal Native American women who wove intricately designed baskets using indigenous plant materials. Traditionally, they had gathered roots and clams in them, stored food in them and even used them for cooking by dropping rocks from the fire into a tightly woven vessel containing food and water. When settlers came, the tribes bartered baskets for iron pots, tools and other goods which they readily put to use.

Educated women who came from the eastern states and from Europe recognized the artistic value of the baskets and began to collect them with a passion. Catering to their taste, Indian women abandoned their durable utilitarian creations for smaller prettier ones which for them were easier and quicker to weave. For the tribes, the baskets became an important source of income.

Another craft that moved from utilitarian to artistic was quilting. The quilting bee was an early form of social life for rural women which justified an escape from isolated housekeeping routines for a sustained get-together with other women. While enjoying friendship and gossip, neighbors helped each other to finish quilts that were both useful and decorative for the owner's home.

As women's lives became more complicated and as ready-made blankets became available, old quilts, like Indian baskets, became collectors' items. Contrary to Victorian speculation, crafts such as quilting, weaving, beadwork and basket-making did not become lost arts. In modern times, they are experiencing a renaissance with frequent exhibits that pair treasured keepsakes with creations by modern artists.

First Native American Woman Novelist

An artist who combined and simultaneously preserved cultural traditions was Mourning Dove (Christal Quintasket) of the Okanogan tribe. As the author of *Cogewea, the Half Breed* (originally published in 1927), she became the first Native American female to write a novel.[1] By interweaving experiences from her own life into the warp and weft of unrecorded legends of her tribe, she preserved in novel form a distinctly Native American perspective. She attracted the attention of Lucullus Virgil McWhorter, a white man of letters, whom the Yakima tribe had adopted as a friend. In addition to mentoring and encouraging her, he edited her work and arranged to have it published.

Mourning Dove was a migrant laborer who had only briefly attended convent and Indian schools. She carried a battered typewriter with her from camp to camp and after long hours in the field, she wrote. At McWhorter's urging, she sought out her Okanogan elders, asking them to tell their tales so that she could record them. She later published *Coyote Stories* to preserve almost forgotten legends and teachings of her tribe.

Although she received invitations to lecture, she rarely accepted them. The recognition, said to have pleased her the most, was her election as an honorary member of the Eastern Washington State Historical Society.

Early Women Artists

During the last quarter of the 19th century, a few women were gaining recognition in the traditionally male European and American art establishment. Among newcomers who made Washington their home were women who had studied at leading art schools and conservatories in Europe, back East and in California. Most were wives and daughters of professional men and, as such, set forth do do their part to civilize their new rough-hewn home towns.

Ida Nowells Cochrane who had studied art in Vienna and New York City introduced an art department to Whitworth College (on its original campus in Tacoma before it moved to Spokane) and later chaired the art

Mourning Dove (Christal Quintasket) of the Okanogans. (Courtesy of the Eastern Washington State Historical Society, Photo #452x)

Emily Inez Denny, daughter of Seattle founders, painting outdoors in a natural setting. She was a protégé of Harriet Beecher and specialized in paintings of pioneer Seattle, Indian scenes, and landscapes of the Puget Sound area. Her works are in the collection of the Historical Society of Seattle and King County. (Courtesy of the Historical Society of Seattle and King County, Neg. #13393)

Abby Williams Hill, her children, and Chief Ta-Tan-Ka-Ska, "White Bull," of the Sioux, whose visits to the Flathead Reservation in Montana coincided. He became their friend, taught them traditional dances and customs, and they in turn taught him English. As a friend of the Indians, she participated in their celebrations and painted their portraits. (Courtesy of Ronald M. Fields, Chairman, Art Department, University of Puget Sound)

As 1909 and Seattle's Alaska-Yukon-Pacific Exposition approached, a group of middle-class black women in Tacoma decided to organize the Clover Leaf Art Club for the express purpose of exhibiting their handiwork at the fair. They won gold, silver and bronze medals for their display of needle and art work. One of the pieces, later presented to the State Historical Society, was Nettie Asberry's handmade opera coat of Battenburg lace which had taken her sister a year to tat.

By far, the best known woman artist in early Washington was Tacoma's Abby Williams Hill who had studied with leading painters of the day at the prestigious Art Students' League of New York City. Starting in the 1890s, Hill received commissions from the State of Washington and from both transcontinental railways to paint landscape scenes, illustrating the beauty of the Northwest. While her husband, Dr. Frank Hill, stayed home, she took her children for lengthy camping trips to Puget Sound islands, the rugged north Cascades, and northwestern Indian reservations. In her "painting tent-studio," she finished each canvas on site.

Both the Great Northern and the Northern Pacific Railroad Companies exhibited her work in other parts of the country to attract tourists and real-estate developers to Washington. Possibly because it was socially unacceptable for a doctor's wife to work for pay, Hill requested only complimentary travel tickets and the return of her paintings which she kept. Despite her achievements, her work was rarely exhibited after 1909. As an artist, she worked alone, seeking neither fame nor profit. In Tacoma, she was probably better known for her involvement in social issues including educational reform through the P.T.A. and advocacy for ethnic minorities and the handicapped. Her son's widow later donated the entire Abby Williams Hill collection to the University of Puget Sound where in recent years it has begun to attract renewed attention.[2]

Women's Art Leagues and Art Clubs

The late 1800s heralded the debut of art leagues and art clubs in communities all over the state. For the most part, members were women, many of whom, like Beecher, Cochrane and Hill, were trained in the arts. In a region where art museums and art institutes were non-existent, the societies not only encouraged local artists; they also enhanced public support and appreciation of art.

A popular notion of the day was that paintings, especially landscapes, had a civilizing, moral influence. By creating order and beauty in the depiction of restless nature, the artist in effect tamed the frontier. In keeping

department at the College of Puget Sound. A graduate of the San Francisco School of Design, Harriet Foster Beecher became one of Puget Sound's best known artists and art instructors. Having come to Seattle to marry Captain Herbert Foote Beecher, she opened an art studio, where wives and daughters of the city's prominent men were her students. She also taught in the art department headed by Katherine D. Allmond at the Territorial University. Later, when the Beechers moved to Port Townsend, she continued her teaching there. When Washington sent 150 paintings to Chicago's World's Columbian Exposition in 1893, 36 were by Beecher and her students.

Group of musicians at the Spokane Interstate Fair, 1914. (Courtesy of the Eastern Washington State Historical Society, Spokane, Photo #L83–18)

with progressivism and reform movements, art also had a political dimension. Its promoters thought that if children could be exposed to fine art and learn to appreciate it, widespread social improvement would eventually result. For art to achieve its potential, it had to be available to everyone, not just the prosperous middle class.

To effect this democratization of art, the Washington Federation of Women's Clubs initiated a program to bring fine art to the public schools. Members donated engravings and reproductions of paintings which they then mounted and framed to place in the buildings. Volunteers visited classrooms and gave "art talks" so that children would understand and appreciate the pictures.

The Spokane Art League

One of Washington's most determined art leagues was in Spokane. Its inception in 1892 resulted directly from a meeting of the state's board of lady managers for the World's Columbian Exposition in Chicago. Spokane business woman, Alice Houghton, headed the board which planned the state's exhibit for the Women's Building and also a women's exhibit for the Washington State Building. One of those in attendance was Julia Widgery Slaughter of Tacoma's Aurora Club who chaired the state's art committee for the exposition. Recognizing the artistic talent of several Spokane women, she suggested that they organize an art league similar to the one in Tacoma.

Under the leadership of Victoria Fellowes, the Spokane Art League (SAL) founded the city's first art school with classes in painting, needle art, wood carving, clay modeling, wainscoating, literature and more. Members also volunteered to teach classes in freehand drawing and modeling in the public schools.

One of the SAL's unique achievements was its identification with the Inland Empire's agricultural community. In 1895, the SAL mounted an expansive exhibit in the Spokesman-Review Building which coincided with Spokane's first Fruit Fair. Along with members' artwork, there was an impressive display of Indian baskets.

In the early 19th century, thousands of people visited the SAL's fine art department at the annual Spokane Interstate Fair. Rural women and the city's ladies of leisure entered their needlework, competing for coveted prizes, while preserving artistic skills that were already threatened by technological advancement. There were numerous categories for all age groups, including oil painting, water color, sculpture, wood carving and more. Blanche Hadley Strong's 1901 winning painting for Best Western Scenery still hangs in the Spokane mayor's offices.

Alice Houghton, Spokane real-estate entrepreneur who owned her own successful business. She chaired Washington State's Board of Lady Managers for the World Columbian Exposition. 1890. (Courtesy of the Spokane Public Library, Northwest Room)

In 1914, Art League patrons reorganized as the Spokane Art Association which continued to sponsor periodic exhibits but no longer offered art classes. For 20 years, the SAL had functioned at the center of Spokane's cultural scene, bringing in outside exhibits and showcasing local work. For the members, it had provided a social and cultural identity along with access for themselves and school children to an art education.

Like the SAL, Tacoma's and Seattle's early art leagues had been dominated by women but reorganized in the mid teens to include more men and to play a less exclusive role within the expanding arts communities. Nonetheless, a number of women's clubs still focused on the visual arts, providing mutual encouragement for members, scholarships for talented young people and patronage for public arts projects.

National League of American Pen Women

In 1927, Armenhouie Lamson called together a group of recognized professional women artists to form a Seattle chapter of the National League of American Pen Women. To be eligible for membership, a woman had to have earned recognition as an author, composer, journalist, poet, artist, architect, historian, etc.—in other words, in a cultural field that involved use of the pen, pencil or brush. Among the first members were Katherine Glen Kerry (composer), Edith Markham Wallace (writer of children's stories), Johanna Freda Greenberg (poet), Sarah Truax Albert (playwrite and actress), Madame Mary Davenport Engberg (composer and conductor), Dorothy Milne Rising (painter and sculptor), and Angie Burt Bowden (historian).

The members participated nationally in contests and exhibitions and also made it a point to honor almost every artist of renown who came to Seattle. Since there were comparatively few Northwest women who met the high standards of the national league, Seattle was at first the only regional chapter. Members sometimes traveled long distances from other parts of the state, so that they could participate. In 1930, Lamson wrote, "Each member has within the last year produced and marketed her wares successfully—books, short and long stories, plays and poems, dramalogues for publication and for radio broadcast . . . also music compositions, lectures, readings, paintings, sculpture, magazine articles, etc."[3]

Among their activities, members offered advice and encouragement to artistic girls and women throughout the Northwest. They frequently served as a clearing house, providing access for non-members to literary markets in the East. The league also founded a junior branch for young people, sponsoring contests and classes and helping talented girls to gain admission to Cornish Institute or other renowned art schools.

Art Museums

Despite the widespread interest in art, Washington was slow to establish major art museums. In 1932, Seattle's Margaret Fuller and her son Dr. Richard Fuller built Seattle an art museum and donated their own impressive collection of Occidental and Oriental treasures. From the start, Dr. Fuller received the credit and was honored as King County's First Citizen. Art patron, Joanna Eckstein, was later asked whether the accolades were appropriately directed. She candidly answered, "Well, originally, I would say it was almost more his mother than it was Dr. Fuller. People seem to have more or less forgotten about her. . . ."[4]

Helen Bailey Murray welcomes the public to the Tacoma Art Museum. Published in the *Tacoma News Tribune*, May 25, 1971. Photo by Wayne Zimmerman. (Courtesy of the *Tacoma News Tribune*)

It was 1971 before Tacoma had a city art museum, again thanks to a woman's vision. When Helen Bailey Murray's husband (lumber mogul L. T. Murray) asked her what she wanted for her birthday, she answered, "I'd like an art museum for Tacoma." Their daughter, Amy Lou Young, and granddaughter, Lowell Anne Butson, fondly recall the story and its importance to their community. Tacoma had long had an art museum organization, but never a suitable building. Wealthy residents who owned valuable art collections would donate them to the Seattle Art Museum or similar facilities to ensure proper care. The Murrays purchased the old bank building from the National Bank of Washington—a three-story brick structure with ample display space and vaults for storage. Following renovation, it was an ideal facility for a downtown art museum. Though not an artist herself, Helen Murray had studied and promoted local arts all her life. She was a charter member of the Tacoma Junior League and a member of the Aloha Club which since the 1880s has been a major patron of the city's arts.

Ladies' Musical Clubs

That there could be a ladies' musical club in every Washington community was the desire of Kate Turner Holmes, turn-of-the-century president of the State Federation of Women's Clubs. Traditionally, women had been excluded from the musical professional establishment where men performed in symphonies and dominated as conductors, composers and soloists.

A ripple effect of the mounting suffrage campaign was women's quest to participate fully in public and professional life, including the arts. In all parts of the country women were forming clubs to develop the musical talent of members and to stimulate musical culture in their communities.

Founded in 1890, the Ladies' Musical Club (LMC) of Tacoma was the first on the west coast, followed the next year by Seattle and then by a host of others. A newcomer to Tacoma, Nellie L. Allyn (wife of Judge Frank Allyn, Sr.) had studied voice in London and Paris. Like many other women who founded western musical clubs, she was an Easterner who deeply missed the cultural environment that she had left behind. Finding other Tacoma women who shared her background and her frustration, she invited them to her home, where they formed an organization. Among its activities, the club established a women's chorus which eventually grew to 100 voices, presenting numerous concerts to S.R.O. audiences in the opulent Tacoma Theatre.

To become a member of an LMC, a woman had to audition; and after she was accepted, she had to perform for other members and/or the public on a regular basis. Accomplished women who lived in rural areas and small towns sometimes travelled long distances, so that they could participate.

In addition to their local involvements, the clubs entered into regional and international competitions. In 1893, Seattle members performed at the Chicago World's Fair, where they were awarded a Diploma for Good Performance. Similarly, the Tacoma LMC chorus won distinctive honors in 1915 at the Panama-Pacific Exposition in San Francisco.

Ladies Musical Club String Quartet

In a series of

CHAMBER MUSIC CONCERTS

WED. EVE. MAR. 2, at 8:15
OLYMPIC HOTEL
Junior Ball Room

Information at Marie Clippinger, Beacon 4016-J2
Tickets on sale at Sherman, Clay.

The Seattle Ladies' Musical Club advertises a performance by this string quartet. 1927. (Courtesy of the Historical Society of Seattle and King County, Photo #18729)

114

Guest Artists Series

At first, club activities consisted of local concerts by members. However, they soon began to reach out, contracting with guest artists to perform in their communities. The early 1900s saw Ladies' Musical Clubs become the chief patrons of musical art in communities throughout the Northwest. Seattle club members sold subscriptions for their annual four-concert Musical Artists Series. For 40 years, Rose Morgenstern Gottstein, the club's concert manager, made her annual trip to New York City where, with a purse of at least $20,000, she negotiated with agents to bring some of the world's foremost musical talents to Seattle. Local audiences flocked to performances by such luminaries as Fritz Kreisler, John McCormack, Madame Ernestine Schumann-Heink, Sergai Rachmaninoff, Alma Gluck and her husband Efram Zimbalist.

When they invited guest artists to perform, the clubs made it a point to include a high percentage of women. Similarly, they supported the professional aspirations of their members. Through peer support, accomplished women enjoyed unprecedented opportunities for public recognition as artists.

Washington's Own Women Virtuosos

The first American woman to compose and conduct a grand opera was Seattle's Mary Carr Moore whose *Narcissa* dramatized the Whitman tragedy. Soloists came from New York's Metropolitan Opera Company with a support cast of 70 local singers, including several of Moore's LMC club sisters. The gala premiere, held in 1912 in the Moore Theatre (owner James Moore was not related to the artist), received high critical acclaim in the local press.[5]

Madame Mary Davenport Engberg, born in a covered wagon near Spokane, rose from humble beginnings to international prominence as a violinist, composer, symphony conductor and teacher. Following five years study in Copenhagen, she moved to Bellingham where, with the help of members of the LMC, she organized and conducted the city's symphony orchestra. Recognized as the first woman to conduct a symphony in America and possibly the world, Engberg later directed the Seattle Civic Orchestra and the Seattle Civic Opera.

Madame Mary Davenport Engberg. 1910. (Courtesy of the Whatcom Museum of History and Art)

Founders of City Symphonies

Like the Bellingham LMC, clubs in other communities took a lead in founding city symphonies. Patsy Bullitt Collins tells of her grandmother, Harriet Overton Stimson, and friends—many of whom were members of the LMC—who sustained the Seattle Symphony in its early years. For the initial performance in 1903, Stimson selected the music and recruited a conductor from New York. Determined that things would be proper, the ladies raided their husbands' closets to borrow formal attire for the musicians. On opening night, Seattle's prominent men sat in the audience in business suits, looking at their coats and tails on the stage.

Progressivism and Music

Karen Blair, Assistant Professor of History at Central Washington University, points out the political implications of the clubs, particularly after World War I.[6] As part of the progressive movement toward a more democratic society, the clubs sought to make good music available to everyone, not just the educated elite. In their efforts to promote musical culture, they launched music education programs for school children and for immigrants.

At the Settlement House, maintained by the Seattle branch of the National Council of Jewish Women, the city's LMC lent its support to a Settlement Music School. Members gave music lessons and organized numerous ensembles of both children and adults. In addition to teaching classical and American music, they encouraged immigrant groups to sing and play their traditional music. It was a give-and-take effort to Americanize the newcomers while encouraging them to preserve and share their cultural heritage.

Demonstrating a love of country, the LMC's introduced serious American composers, Negro spirituals, folk songs and patriotic hymns to the concert repertoire which had traditionally been European. Their efforts strengthened the public role of women while challenging the priorities of the white male establishment.

Focus on Ethnic Music

At a time when there was little fraternizing between people of different races, white LMC's took it upon themselves to discover and present indigenous music. The network of clubs thrilled to new breakthroughs which they publicized far and wide.

Vera Jane Edwards (seated third from right) played the part of Minnehaha in her company's romanticized performance of the "Wedding Fete" at a Seattle theater in 1912. The event was a benefit for the YWCA Industrial Clubs. (YWCA of Seattle/King County Records, University of Washington Libraries)

When the Tacoma Club presented its "Costume Concert of American Indian Music," reviews reached the European press. The stage set at the Tacoma Theatre resembled an Indian camp in a forest. Members of the LMC wore bonafide Indian regalia on loan from Alice Palmer Henderson's famed collection. According to the program, their songs and dances were based on "authenticated" tribal melodies. Club members most likely were unaware of the sharp contrast between their romanticized portrayal and the realities of life on nearby reservations. There, children were punished if they spoke Indian words in school and traditional tribal celebrations were severely restricted.

116

State Federation of Colored LMC's

For a number of years, the State Federation of Colored LMC's held its separate annual convention. In black churches and community centers, members gave music lessons and performed a wide range of classical and traditional music. Finally in 1936, three members of the Colored LMC of Tacoma participated in the general convention of Washington LMC's held in Walla Walla. Doris Bowling gave a paper on "Negro Folk Music" while Minnie Gilbert Elmore and Madelyn Roberts Gibson sang a medley of Negro spirituals.

Today many of Washington's communities continue to prosper from the influence of ladies' musical societies. As non-profit organizations, they provide scholarships to assist promising young musicians. In addition they lend their support to other worthwhile organizations in their communities, such as symphonies or social service agencies. Many of the clubs still sponsor recitals by guest artists. Active members maintain their high musical standards, performing for each other and for the public.

Cornish Institute

Like many women of her day, Nellie Centennial Cornish (her middle name referred to 1876, the year of her birth) had grown up in a poor family without benefit of a formal education. Following repeated financial failures, the family moved from Nebraska to Oregon and finally to Blaine, each time seeking a fresh start and a change of fortune. Nellie Cornish got her first break in 1900, when she was hired to sell musical instruments in Seattle. She later turned to teaching piano and in 1914 joined with other music instructors to form her first Cornish School in a rented studio. When neighbors objected to the noise and sued to have the school closed, the judge suggested to the plaintiffs that they move to the country.

Women's post-war enthusiasm for the arts resulted in the founding of several of the nation's major arts institutes. In Seattle, patrons contributed generously, so that in 1921 Cornish School moved into its permanent home. Florence Bean James who joined the faculty as theater director described the building. "I was enchanted by my first glimpse of Cornish school. It was situated on the corner of a tree lined street in a residential area. The architecture was something called Spanish baroque, unique in itself and different from anything else in the city. It was peach-colored stucco, trimmed in sage green, with touches of dog-wood as the decorative motif. Unmistakably, it was a school of the arts. The school had been carefully planned to provide adequate facilities for all arts . . . best of all, there was a lovely small theatre seating around 300."[7]

Tacoma Young Ladies Musical Club (young black women) perform at Allen African Methodist Episcopal Church. 1934. (Courtesy of the Tacoma Public Library, Northwest Room)

Nellie Centennial Cornish. (Courtesy of Spec. Collections Div., Univ. of Washington Libraries, Neg. #862)

117

From the beginning, Cornish School had programs for young people. This photo is from an advertisement for Cornish, placed in the 1916 Broadway High School year book. (Courtesy of Seattle Public Schools Archives)

Nellie Cornish envisioned a school where students could experience the interrelatedness of the arts and as her institute matured, her vision became a reality. Students could study all branches of music, drama, the visual arts and dance, along with supplemental subjects such as costuming and set design. In keeping with efforts to democratize the arts, Miss Cornish maintained that creativity should be developed in the average person, as well as the talented, and further, that art's ultimate purpose was enrichment for everyone—not just the privileged elite.

With an uncanny instinct for quality and originality, she hired both famous and unknown artists for her faculty. Before he had gained even local recognition, she invited Mark Tobey to teach painting in his own manner. Sensing an enormous and unusual talent, she arranged a solo performing debut for one of her avant-garde dance instructors, Martha Graham. When white Russian intellectuals and artists fled their homeland via the Orient in 1917, her intuition told her to offer them teaching positions.

Reflecting on how her dream had finally become a reality, Miss Cornish wrote, "It is because not one person, but many have brought their pet dreams together, and have made it a home for ideals. All work, not for me, nor for themselves, but for the artistic ideals of the school."[8]

Known affectionately to her students as Miss Aunt Nellie, she often invited her students to meet informally with famous guest artists over coffee and home-baked cookies in her apartment. She also was quick to help with tuition costs, since she thought it wrong for artists to have to justify themselves economically. On one occasion, a friend found her tearing up IOU's and was outraged at the students' ingratitude, since only a few ever managed to repay their loans. Responding philosophically, Nellie Cornish said, "Well, I've thought a lot about gratitude. It's like a muscle. If it isn't exercised it atrophies. You just have to learn to exercise gratitude every day of your life to stay alive."[9] With wealthy benefactors who repeatedly bailed her school out of debt, she could afford to exercise her gratitude.

Had it not been for friends including Jeannette Whitimore Skinner, Mrs. A. H. Anderson, Harriet Overton Stimson, Edgar Ames and others, Cornish Institute might not have survived the Great Depression. An organization of women called the Seattle Music and Art Foundation also lent its support and in the 1950s assumed ownership of the school to put it on an even financial keel.

Today the school is managed by a board of both men and women and according to president Jeannette Edris Rockefeller, its financial condition is excellent. In recent years, Cornish Institute has expanded its facilities adding new subjects to the curriculum to become one of four accredited schools of visual and performing arts in the country. Of those, it is the only one supported completely by private funding.

Little Theatre and Children's Theatre

Following the Armistice and the passage of the 19th Amendment, the roaring twenties unleashed a nation-wide explosion of women's creative energies. Drama Leagues and Schools of Allied Arts gained footing in Washington cities. The state also benefited from the influence of Cornish Institute whose faculty and programs were at the forefront of American theater.

In 1918, Nellie Cornish lured Ellen Van Volkenburg and her husband Maurice Browne—founders of the Little Theatre Movement in America—from Chicago to her school. She promised them a free hand in developing a drama department in accord with their philosophy which was "that the final test of civilization is its art; that all arts meet, attain their highest development and are fused in the art of theater."[10] To the Cornish curriculum the Brownes added playwriting, staging and acting. They also established a local theater where students honed their skills, sharing the stage with professional actors.

When Ellen Van Volkenburg and her husband divorced, he left Seattle and she remained. In addition to her work at Cornish, she helped develop the Tacoma Little Theatre where she was director, producer and actress in several plays. Thirty years later, Tacoma's Association of Business and Professional Women presented its annual Woman of Achievement Award to Helen Weed. Weed, who had served as long-term executive secretary/manager of the TLT, was credited as the major reason for its success and financial soundness.

Florence Bean James took over direction of the Cornish drama department in the mid-1920s. While she taught acting and directed plays, her husband, Burton, trained students to design and construct sets. The Jameses went on to found the Seattle Repertory Playhouse, a professional theater which staged plays for both adult and child audiences.

In Seattle, Lois Beil Sandall had pioneered children's theater. She began in 1918 by recruiting drama students from the University of Washington to perform plays at Plymouth Congregational Church. A year later she founded the Players' Art Guild staffed entirely by volunteers who produced three plays a year. In 1923, the troupe gained backing from the city's Drama League to produce plays especially for children.

Sandall declared, "Plays just for children are a vital need in Seattle. Not movies, nor puppets, but plays to appeal to the child imagination, depicted by adult actors, with all their sympathy, skill and understanding of the child's heart. I have been preparing for just such a moment, and have

The Tacoma Drama League of 1926 later became the Tacoma Little Theater. This performance of "Cassile's Engagement" by John Hankin was a comedy, directed by Ellen Van Volkenburg. Tacoma teacher and actress, Elsa Nessenson, (third from left on the couch) received rave reviews for her portrayal of Mrs. Borridge. (Courtesy of the Tacoma Public Library, Northwest Room)

in readiness a number of plays adaptable to children's theater."[11] Enthusiastic support for the children's plays came from the YWCA, Cornish Institute, the Plymouth Girls' Club and the Women's University Club, all of which sponsored performances in their auditoriums.

In the mid-1930s, Florence James carried children's theater to audiences throughout the state. The Great Depression had fallen hard on Washington's communities where unemployment statistics rose to some of the highest in the nation. Governor Clarence Martin was quick to take advantage of President Franklin D. Roosevelt's New Deal programs and to solicit other outside support to bolster the flagging economy. Consequently, Washington fared better than most other states as it emerged from the crisis.

Among the programs to put people back to work was the WPA Federal Theatre Project, organized and directed locally by Florence James. As part of the project, she started Washington's first all-black acting company in Seattle. Sara Oliver Jackson, who starred in some of the Negro Reperatory Theatre's productions, considers it the best time she could have had as a young person. She says that black actors were able to bring details of black culture into the plays which attracted large audiences.

119

Russian immigrants brought with them a colorful tradition of children's theater. Maria Rychkoff of Seattle's St. Spiradon Cathedral-Orthodox Church served as director, while Galina Gorohoff designed and painted the elaborate sets. Performances were held at St. Spiradon, the Masonic Temple and the Women's Century Club. Ca. 1930. (Courtesy of Marina Pavlovna Reva Dietsch)

James also created the WPA touring drama company that brought classic plays to high school students throughout the state. Supervised by the State Department of Education, the program received funding from the Rockefeller Foundation to become the first state theater in America. In rural communities, the troupe often played to S.R.O. audiences, made up of bus-loads of young people, whom the school districts transported from miles around. With the ebb of the Depression in the late 1930s, both the Negro Theatre and the young people's drama company lost their federal funding, but both left as their legacy a lasting impact on the region's cultural growth.

During the same period, Seattle's Violet Lucks read a magazine article about an organization in New York City called Junior Programs which mounted plays for children and toured them throughout the country. She and others who shared her interest succeeded in drawing performances to the Northwest. The outbreak of World War II ended the liaison with New York, but the group of Seattle women who had formed a local Junior Programs board was determined to continue. Looking at uprooted families that crowded into make-shift communities around The Boeing Company and nearby military bases, the group felt that plays and cultural linkages were more important than ever for the children.

The board launched a membership drive, raised funds and hired Florence James as the first director—the organization's only paid position. Members contacted schools in western Washington, rented halls, sold tickets, handed out printed programs and ushered children to their seats. According to Dottie Simpson, a Junior Programs president, performances were attended by some 16,000 children per year. In 1984 Simpson said, "I know that many of our theater-goers today, and many of our arts patrons, attended Junior Programs and got hooked on the arts at a young age. The experience turned them into theater people."

The board established a close working relationship with the University of Washington's Department of Drama where Junior Programs paid the first year's salary for two new women faculty members one of whom specialized in children's drama and the other in creative dramatics. In addition, membership dues supported scholarships for students of children's drama.

Junior Programs activities continued into the 1970s. According to Simpson, the group's demise came about in part because of Title III which toured professional drama troupes to elementary schools throughout the country. Another reason was the board's insistence on remaining debt free and relying on volunteer actors. Board members had successfully pushed for a bond issue to build a permanent theater as part of the Seattle World's Fair. While the women wanted the theater to remain non-profit, a group that was predominantly men promoted the idea of a professional theater company with paid actors and staff. With the prospect of increased professional opportunity, local actors were less willing to volunteer.

Simpson speculates that if Junior Programs had been willing to change, it might well have survived as the region's premiere children's theater. As in the past, many of the women who were involved continue to participate in guilds that raise funds to support the arts, including professional theater.

Japanese Traditional Arts

Japanese-American pioneers were often well educated with an appreciation for traditional arts. In communities throughout Washington, immigrant women strove to sustain their traditions both as artists and as teachers of younger generations. Teiko Tomita labored with her husband in the fields and cared for the family in their primitive home near Wapato. Despite hard work and isolation from other Japanese women, she composed *tanka*. The brief, lyrical poems are an ancient Japanese means of expressing innermost feelings in the context of day-to-day observations. In later years, when the family moved to Sunnydale (now SeaTac International Airport), Tomita joined a Tanka Club in Seattle which submitted her prize-winning poems to be published in Japan.[12]

In other Washington communities, Japanese women's clubs focused on traditional poetry, flower arranging, dance and the ancient tea ceremony. In addition to practicing the arts themselves, members patiently taught them to children. The clubs built and sustained community life and were a source of strength during times of intense race discrimination. Gail Nomura, Director of the Asian/Pacific American Studies Program at Washington State University, cites the Yakima Japanese Poetry Club as an example. The club taught children to read traditional literature. Eventually, a baseball club grew out of the reading class, drawing the whole Japanese American community together for Sunday afternoon games and recreation.

In 1909, when Seattle hosted the Alaska-Yukon-Pacific Exposition, the city's "Japantown" was experiencing its own cultural awakening. Perhaps it was the Japanese government's extravagant participation in the AYP that prompted the local community to build its own Nippon Kan (Japanese Hall). Perhaps it was the influx of wives, many of whom were schooled in traditional dance and music. Or perhaps it was a proud reaction to Seattle's theaters which restricted non-whites to balcony seats. In any case, the

Teiko Tomita, Wapato, 1921. (The photo appeared in the "Yakima Valley Japanese American Pioneers" photo exhibit curated by Gail M. Nomura, Director, Asian/Pacific American Studies Program and Assistant Professor, Department of Comparative American Cultures and Department of American History, Washington State University)

Nippon Kan filled a void and became a highly valued community center where families enjoyed traditional dance, theater, political debates, demonstrations of the martial arts, visiting evangelists and more.

Tama Tokuda, who studied dance at the school, recalls the precision of the instruction and the careful preparation that preceded a performance. One of her teachers was Madame Nakatani who had learned to teach the exacting classical dance through a traditional apprenticeship in Japan. Her entire repertoire was committed to memory and students learned by watching, then imitating her. She taught one student at a time, playing the samisen herself to accompany them while they danced.

For students and their families, classical dance was a serious commitment. Pupils went from the public school to the Japanese school and then to their dance class, often arriving home after dark. Recitals at the Nippon Kan were family oriented and an important part of community life. The Nippon Kan flourished until 1942, when west coast Japanese Americans were evacuated inland to internment camps during World War II. After 1942, the Nippon Kan remained closed for 39 years. Thanks to the efforts of Edward and Elizabeth Burke, it was recently restored and once again stages Kabuki dramas and Japanese dance performances.

Like the Japanese Americans, other ethnic groups have retained traditional arts and customs, largely through the efforts of women. While trying to assimilate into the American culture, immigrant women have endeavored to keep younger generations in touch with their roots, teaching children traditional songs, dances and other arts. Today Washington State is one of the most culturally diverse in the nation. As a result, its communities boast an abundant cultural heritage with a variety of ethnic festivals and events to showcase a smorsgasbord of traditional arts.

Notes

1. Hum-Ishu-Ma, "Mourning Dove," *Cogewea, the Half-Blood,* Intro. by Dexter Fisher, (University of Nebraska Press, 1981).
2. See Ronald M. Fields, *Abby Rhoda Wiliams Hill, 1861–1943: Northwest Frontier Artist,* to be published during the 1989 Washington State Centennial by the Washington State Historical Society, Tacoma. Fields is chairman of the Art Department at the University of Puget Sound and, as such, has charge of Hill collection.
3. Armenhouie Lamson, President, National League of American Pen Women, Seattle, Annual Report, 1930.
4. Joanna Eckstein, Oral history interview, University of Washington Manuscripts Collection.
5. See Catherine Parsons Smith and Cynthia S. Richardson, *Mary Carr Moore, American Composer,* (Ann Arbor, 1987).
6. See Karen J. Blair, "The Seattle Ladies' Musical Club, 1890–1930," in *Women in Pacific Northwest History: an Anthology* (Seattle, 1988).
7. Florence Bean James papers, University of Washington Manuscripts Collection.
8. Nellie Cornish, *The Autobiography of Miss Aunt Nellie* (Seattle, 1964), p. xiii.
9. ibid.
10. Adele M. Ballard, "A Real Dramatic School for Seattle and Western Washington," *The Town Crier,* 7, (Seattle, Jan., 1919), p. 7.
11. "Mrs. Robert Sandall," *Seattle Woman,* I, no. 2 (June, 1923), p. 14.
12. See Gail Nomura, "Tsugiki, a Grafting: a History of Japanese Pioneer Woman in Washington State, in Karen J. Blair, ed. *Women in Pacific Northwest History: an Anthology* (Seattle, 1988).

Bhuddist girls with fans and musical instruments posed in front of Tacoma temple. Photo by Boland. (Courtesy of the Tacoma Public Library, Northwest Room)

The new Seattle, Lake Shore and Eastern Railroad linked the waterfront with the east side of Lake Washington and eventually reached Snoqualmie Falls, where the owners dropped their original plan to extend the line through the Cascades to Spokane. Such transportation enabled women to take a more active role in community development and to attend meetings at city hall. Photo by Asahel Curtis. (Courtesy of Special Collections Div., Univ. of Washington Libraries, A. Curtis photo #59932)

124

Preservation

8

Fueling the burgeoning national women's club movement of the late 19th century was a passion for literary culture, environmentalism, and historic preservation. While only a select number of women had had the privilege of a college education, others with increased leisure time wanted the opportunity to learn and to participate. Their clubs paved the way.

At club meetings, women made contact with the literary culture of the day, enjoying opportunities to read, discuss, and broaden their horizons. In addition to literature, their programs focused on art, music, history, the environment, and personal improvement.

Collectively and as individuals, early Washington women were actively involved in community development, serving with men on boards and committees to plan public parks and playground areas, as well as museums and libraries.

Public Libraries

In 1896, when club women organized the Washington State Federation of Women's Clubs, one of their initial projects was the outfitting of travelling libraries to send to rural and book-starved communities. In addition, club members joined forces to agitate for more and better libraries at both the state and local levels.

Washington's library movement had its antecedents in the 1860s, when upstanding men and women in several of the territory's rough-hewn communities established organizations to foster "mental culture." They met frequently for lectures, discussion and literary entertainment, while raising funds to purchase materials for public reading rooms.

In Seattle, Sarah Yesler (wife of the first mayor) was the first librarian, while Catherine Maynard (wife of the city's first doctor) provided a reading room in her home. As the community grew and life became more complex, the men gradually withdrew and the original library association was dissolved. In the late 1880s, a group of prominent community women revitalized the program by forming the Ladies' Library Association which set forth with determination to salvage this vital part of their city's early cultural life.

When Seattle citizens ratified their city charter in 1890, it included a provision for a public library department to be governed by five commissioners, at least two of whom had to be women. The stipulation was due in part to recognition of the efforts of community women, but also to the attitude of the commissioners who in their first report ranked the library "among the luxuries of civilized life."

Members of the Everett Book Club costumed themselves for a Colonial Tea Party held at the Monte Cristo Hotel in 1895. The club founded the city's public library. (Courtesy of the Everett Public Library).

Spokane Public Library director, Mr. Fuller, poses with his staff for this Christmas card photo. (Courtesy of the Spokane Public Library, Northwest Room).

Similarly, women's organizations in communities all over the state rallied to the late 19th century challenge to promote literary culture. The Ladies Educational Aid Society in Dayton, the Women's Reading Club in Walla Walla, the Women's Library Society in Tacoma, the Woman's Club of Olympia, and the Woman's Book Club in Everett all worked to establish public libraries in their communities. In Ellensburg, Catherine Murray, a member of the Ladies' Municipal Improvement Society, donated two lots for the site of the future library, while members of the Friday and Gallina Clubs helped to raise funds for books.

Efforts to garner funds and facilities were sometimes ingenious and on other occasions ill-conceived. The Yakima Women's Christian Temperance Union, which had established the community's first public reading room, promoted ambitious building plans for a temple to house a library, lecture hall, and offices. When the dream failed to capture citizen support, the WCTU abandoned its project, whereupon community women, under the leadership of Susanna Steinweg, regrouped to organize the North Yakima Library Association. As in other communities, the women sponsored events, such as box socials, spelling bees, dances and concerts by members to raise funds for books. They took turns acting as librarian in the reading room, which was located in the office of the county superintendent of schools.

In the mill town of Port Madison, women also rallied to found a library association. The community was changing, due in part to an 1882 law that required a "squaw man" to either marry his Native American concubine or give her up. In a rowboat, the sheriff went from camp to camp, performing marriage ceremonies. When a man chose not to marry, he had to give the Indian woman money and whatever she wanted from their house, whereupon the sheriff took her to the nearest reservation and put her ashore. In the itinerant community, where Indian and non-Indian women alike followed their husbands from one camp to another, the first libraries and schools brought a new sense of stability.

Typically, as fledgling libraries grew and began to attract public support, the women's organizations presented them as a gift to their communities. Likewise, the Washington State Federation of Women's Clubs presented its traveling library system to the State Library Commission which

Sarah Yesler was librarian in Seattle's first reading room and a founding member of the Ladies' Library Association. Following her death, her husband, Henry, donated their mansion to the city for a public library. When it burned to the ground in 1901, the ladies managed to salvage many of the books. (Courtesy of Paul Dorpat).

Downtown Seattle's Carnegie Library was erected at Fourth and Madison in 1906. (Courtesy of the Seattle Public Library).

was established at the turn of the century. The original commissioners were the State Superintendent of Public Instruction, the presidents of the University of Washington and Washington State College, one member recommended by the WSFWC, and two members appointed by the governor, one of whom had to be a woman. One of the members was Seattle's Kate Turner Holmes, president of the WSFWC, who reported that the commission's initial work consisted of enlarging and improving the traveling library system.

With successive gubernatorial administrations, the structure of the library commission changed, so that women gradually lost their clout. New commissioners were largely figureheads who had little time to concern themselves with libraries. For instance, at one time the entire membership was made up of justices of the state's Supreme Court. Nonetheless, the WSFWC continued to keep its finger on the pulse of the commission, scheduling conferences with the members, lobbying the legislature for improvements, and doing its best to provide information to the public.

While the state commission fell victim to political whims, libraries in many Washington communities gained new vigor, thanks to generous gifts from Andrew Carnegie. Modestly, clubwomen stepped back, while male community leaders congratulated themselves and took the credit for their stately new buildings and expanded collections. However, library work had a history of being "women's work." Partially because of this and partially because they acknowledged the contributions of clubwomen, councilmen often invited women to continue to participate in their library's governance. In modern times, Washington women have strong representation on library boards at local, county and state levels.

Historic Preservation

In their organizations, their families, and their ethnic groups, women have commonly assumed responsibility for the preservation of historic and cultural traditions.

From guards wearing Prussian helmets to women crowned with mortarboards, this Fourth of July parade in Burlington appears to have had a unique theme. 1907. Photo by Caswell's Studio. (Courtesy of the Skagit County Historical Museum)

Daughters of the American Revolution

Determined to perpetuate patriotism and the memory of their ancestors, a group of women met in the 1890s to organize nationally as the Daughters of the American Revolution. Members had to be descendents of veterans who won the war for independence. Of particular interest to the founders were the heroines of the war, most of whom had already fallen into obscurity. Many of the local and state chapters are named after them.

In Washington State, the DAR sponsored a competition to design the official state flag. When University of Washington history professor, Edmond Meany, decided that a statue of George Washington should greet visitors to the Alaska-Yukon-Pacific Exposition, he turned to the Rainier Chapter of the DAR. Among its schemes to raise $20,000 for the project, the DAR declared Washington's Birthday as Monument Day, asking school children all over the state to contribute one, but not more than five pennies. Today, visitors still pose for pictures with the heroic bronze statue that since 1909 has maintained its vigil at an entrance to the university campus.

In the wake of World War I, Ellensburg's Jean Schnebly Davidson, chair of the state DAR's Preservation of Historic Spots Committee, mailed an ambitious agenda to other regents. From chapters all over the state, she requested biographical sketches of pioneers and lists of their personal possessions that might still exist. She also asked for accounts of homes, buildings, and important events. Among its activities, the DAR placed markers on spots that it considered historically significant.

The founders of the DAR chapter in Ellensburg were Leta May and Clareta Olmstead Smith—dedicated local historians who amassed a significant archival collection, relating to the Kittitas valley. Included are traditionally neglected subjects, especially agricultural and women's history. The sisters preserved their grandparents' log cabin on the family homestead and created a living pioneer farm, which they donated to the state as a park. A local attraction for tourists and school children alike, the Olmstead Place was added to the National Register of Historic Places.

Daughters of the Pioneers of Washington

The Smith sisters were also linked to the Daughters of the Pioneers of Washington whose forebears had to have been in the territory prior to 1870. The organization, founded in Seattle in 1911, met in Sarah Loretta Denny Hall (also called Pioneer Hall), which Denny had presented to the Pioneer Society the previous year. Current member Claire Rahm speculates that the women may have felt a need for their own sphere apart from male pioneers, so that they could proceed with ambitious projects of their own in historic preservation.

The members began to collect and publish the biographies of their own pioneer ancestors. They also established a library to collect and preserve the state's history, biography, fiction, folklore, and Native American heritage. Housed first in the Hall of Justice in Olympia and later in the State Historical Society's archives in Tacoma, the collection has been a valuable asset for researchers. Among their accomplishments, the Daughters of the Pioneers promoted successful legislation to require the public schools and state teachers' colleges to include mandatory courses in Washington State history and government.

In cooperation with other women's clubs and historical societies, they worked to restore landmark structures and to mark historic sites. The Bellingham chapter refurbished the home built by Captain George E. Pickett and his Native American wife in 1856; the Olympia chapter restored the Nathaniel Crosby home in Tumwater; the Pasco chapter was instrumental

Fourth of July picnic at the Judson's old homestead, Lynden, 1893. A covered-wagon pioneer, Phoebe Judson set up household in the midst of the forest, where she mothered her own four children, along with orphaned children of Indian women. She helped to establish the first church and school, gave political speeches in the 1880s, and served on school boards and juries. She marched to the polls with her husband, a staunch Democrat, and voted the Republican ticket. At the age of 95, she wrote and published her memoirs in a popular book entitled *A Pioneer's Search for an Ideal Home*. (Courtesy of the Center for Pacific Northwest Studies)

in commemorating the spot at the confluence of the Columbia and Snake Rivers, visited by Lewis and Clark in 1803; and the Seattle chapter helped the Suquamish community to build a replica of the tribe's former Ole Man House which honored Chief Sealth (Seattle). Several chapters helped to research and preserve the legacy of early Hudson Bay and Northwest Company fur traders at Fort Walla Walla, Fort Vancouver, Spokane House, Fort Simcoe (Yakima), Fort Nisqually (near Steilacoom and Tacoma), and others.

Museums and Historical Societies

In 1908, when the Ferry Museum (now the Washington State Historical Society) needed larger quarters, Tacoma's newly organized Presidents' Council of Women's Organizations launched a funding drive to raise an $8,000 donation for a new building. In 1925, Spokane's Helen Campbell Powell gave her opulent girlhood home to the Eastern Washington State Historical Society as a memorial to her mother, Grace Campbell. In 1939, Olympia's Mary Elizabeth Reynolds Lord donated the Lord Mansion to the state, stipulating that it should become the State Capital Historical Museum.

In Seattle, the process of acquiring an historical museum was more tedious. On November 13, 1911, the 60th anniversary of the arrival of the city's first settlers, Emily Carkeek, a transplanted Englishwoman with a strong sense of heritage, invited several women friends to a Founders' Day luncheon to discuss forming an organization devoted to local history. Costumed in pioneer clothing, the ladies dined on a chowder made from Puget Sound butter clams.

The elegant Carkeek mansion, built by Emily's husband, Morgan, subsequently became the setting for annual Founders' Day luncheons, resulting in the formal incorporation of the Seattle and King County Historical Society in 1914. Initially, members formed committees to research local history and to gather artifacts and memorabilia, which they stored in a fireproof building at the University of Washington.

Until her death in 1926, Emily Carkeek led the society—which included both men and women—in its search for a museum site. Ten years later, the Carkeeks' only daughter Guendolen Plestcheeff was elected president and served until 1952, when her mother's dream finally came true. Thanks to the legacy of the Founders' Day parties, Seattle's Museum of History and Industry, located on the Lake Washington ship canal at the north end of the Arboretum, has one of the largest collections on the West Coast.

The Thomas Burke Memorial Washington State Museum also owes much of its heritage to women. On her death in 1925, Caroline McGilvra Burke left a substantial bequest to establish an appropriate monument to the life and work of her late husband, Judge Thomas Burke. Her will directed that the funds be used for ". . . the erection . . . of a building to advance the cause of a better mutual understanding between . . . the peoples of the Pacific shores." A pioneer member of Seattle's emerging establishment, she was a socialite, philanthropist, and world traveler, who had donated her own substantial collections—most notably of northwest Native American artifacts—to the Washington State Museum.

That museum's precursor was the Society of Young Naturalists, founded in Seattle in the 1880s. From the beginning, women were involved, gleaning the seashores and forests to gather specimens of insects, plants, shells, etc. for the society's collection. While such activity was popular at the time, the Young Naturalists, whose members included professors from the Territorial University, pursued it with scientific zeal, carefully categorizing and preserving each new find. As the acquisitions grew, the museum expanded its focus so that under the directorship of anthropologist, Erna Gunther, it became a leading center for the study of the culture, history and art of Native Americans on the Northwest Coast.

When its aging building, located on the University of Washington campus, was condemned in the 1950s, a logical solution was to combine Caroline Burke's memorial to her husband with the financially strapped museum. After considerable debate about expanding the mission and changing the name, designated in 1899 by the State Legislature, financial considerations won out with a compromise moniker of "Thomas Burke Memorial Washington State Museum."

Ethnic, Immigrant and Religious Women

Not all women were eligible for membership in the DAR and the Daughters of the Pioneers which, like the federated women's clubs, were predominantly white and Protestant. Through their families, churches and secular organizations, other women also strove to preserve their past. Long before black history was taught in schools, black women's clubs did their homework, highlighting role models to influence their children and keeping alive their traditional music, folk stories and other cultural traditions. In Washington State, they collected stories of black people, especially women, who had made a difference. Through black women's clubs and churches, black children learned about their history.

Members of the Seattle Historical Society dressed in pioneer costumes for their annual Founder's Day party at the Carkeek Mansion. Emily Carkeek is second from right in the front row. Ca. 1911. (Courtesy of the Historical Society of Seattle and King County)

Caroline McGilvra Burke (seated on the railing in white) poses with Native American guests on the porch of the Burke mansion. (Courtesy of Special Collections Div., University of Washington Libraries, UW Neg. #905)

The Sisters of Providence, who are mandated by their charter to record their history, have amassed an impressive collection. Located in Seattle, their archives include notebooks that date back to 1856, when Mother Joseph and her little band of nuns arrived at Fort Vancouver. In her native French, the Sister Chronicler penned her observations of daily events, including the trivial along with milestones.

Mother Frances Xavier Cabrini of another Catholic order was an Italian immigrant, who founded 67 institutions throughout the nation. During the final 14 years of her life, she lived and worked in Seattle. Her last project was the city's Columbus Sanitarium which became Columbus Hospital and was later renamed St. Cabrini Hospital in her honor. After her death in 1917 in Chicago, Mother Cabrini was canonized as the Catholic Church's first American saint and patroness of immigrants. Her name is the first engraved on a special plaque at the feet of the Statue of Liberty. It seems appropriate that her last work was in Washington State which has one of the most ethnically diverse populations in the nation.

Noted for her philanthropy, Caroline Burke had many interests, including world travel, Native American artifacts, and posing for photographers. Photo by Edward Curtis. (Courtesy of Special Collections Div., University of Washington Libraries, UW Neg. #2729)

Here members of Everett's Vasa Sewing Club pose with American and Norwegian flags on a 1930s parade float. (Courtesy of the Everett Public Library).

Juanita Barron and her granddaughter Juanita. In the early 1950s, when the family migrated from Texas to Toppenish, Señora Barron worked in the fields along with her husband and 13 children, until the family later moved to Seattle. Although she could neither read nor write, she provided a cultural anchor, making sure that the children spoke Spanish and maintaining her altar. Her son Roger, now a Seattle elementary school principal, says, "That sort of support has kept our community together." Seattle, 1984. Photo by Bob Haft. (Courtesy of the Chicano Archives, the Evergreen State College Library)

The Wapato Girls Club. 1929. (This photo appeared in the "Yakima Valley Japanese American Pioneers" photo exhibit curated by Gail M. Nomura, Director, Asian/Pacific American Studies Program and Assistant Professor, Department of Comparative American Cultures and Department of History, Washington State University.)

For immigrant women, many of whom did not speak English, treasured keepsakes and remembrances of family and friends in the old country were often an anchor in a storm of difficult readjustment. Many had come with starry-eyed dreams of an America, where everything would be better and more beautiful than at home. One Chinese woman had envisioned streets paved with gold.

For a few, the dreams came true. Annine Harder married at a young age and immigrated from Schlesswig-Holstein to the rocky steppes near Sprague. She worked with her husband to amass huge holdings of the largely untillable land which no one else wanted. Livestock grazed on the native grasses and eventually Harder became matriarch of one of the nation's largest cattle ranches. Most immigrant women were not so fortunate and their dreams quickly shattered in the face of hardship and alienation in a foreign land. As they gradually began the process of cultural assimilation, they strove to preserve traditions and memories that they valued.

Women from Japan sometimes lived in cities, but were often isolated on farms in rural areas. As soon as their time and their proximity to each other allowed, they formed Ikebana (flower arranging) and Tanka (poetry)

Chinese Consul and merchant Goon Dip arrived with his wife in Portland in 1885 and later moved to Seattle. Here, she poses with her daughter, Martha, and son, Daniel. In accord with Chinese tradition, her primary obligation was to her home and family and she was rarely seen in public. When she appeared at official functions, she maintained an aristocratic bearing, often wearing the color yellow to symbolize her high station. Her children and grandchildren became leaders in the local Chinese community, where they preserved valuable cultural traditions. One that they did not preserve was the bound feet, seen here, peeking out from beneath the mother's skirt. (Courtesy of the Willard Jue Estate)

There were men from the Philippines in the Northwest as early as the 1880s, but only a few women immigrated prior to 1920. Here Josefa Espiritu Diaz Barrazona (front row, right) poses with her graduating class in 1923 at Kirkland's NW Training School for Christian women. A widow, she came to Seattle to join her brothers. According to historian, Fred Cordova, the first Pinays served to stabilize the Filipino community, reminding the men of families they had left behind. (Courtesy of Demonstration Project for Asian Americans. Published in: Fred Cordova, *Filipinos: Forgotten Asian Americans*, Dubuque, 1983)

Children from 24 different nationalities pose for their class photo in Roslyn. n.d. (Courtesy of the Ellensburg Public Library)

clubs which, in addition to preserving traditional arts, offered instruction to their daughters. Japanese Girls' Clubs, such as the one in Wapato, were a sort of finishing school, where older women instructed girls in the arts and taught them to perform the ancient tea ceremony.

Similarly, women of other ethnic groups have formed organizations to help each other and their community and to preserve their heritage. Some of the older ones are the Seattle Council of Jewish Women, the Daughters of Norway and the Vasa Lodges, the Slovenian Women's Lodge in Tacoma, and Fidelia Clubs for Italian women. By the 1930s, there were clubs for Chinese and Filipino women. Other women, such as Russians, Greeks and Volga Germans, worked predominantly through their churches, where they also preserved their cultural traditions.

One of the most ethnically diverse rural communities in Washington State is Roslyn on the eastern slope of the Cascades, where waves of black miners from the southern states and immigrants from Italy and eastern Europe came to work in the coal mines. It was a hard life, frought with

mining disasters and complicated by a polyglot of languages among many groups that did not speak English. There were numerous organizations in the town, including black women's clubs and the Druidessa Lodge for Italian women. Most other ethnic women did not have organizations of their own, but on special occasions, such as weddings, holiday celebrations and frequent funerals, they prepared traditional food and participated at their husbands' lodges.

In the community with its large bachelor population, life was especially hard for uneducated European wives who often had little opportunity or time for contact with other women. An example is a Croatian woman whose name has been forgotten. She came (probably ca. 1890) as a picture bride for an arranged marriage to a man who squandered his earnings in taverns, beat her and insisted on keeping her pregnant. When he died, she was left with several children, no knowledge of English, and about $200 which she received as a death benefit.

She used the money for a down payment on a house and went to work, cleaning other people's homes and taking in laundry—mostly miners' filthy work clothes. An enterprising home economist, she planted a huge vegetable garden, bought pigs, a cow and some chickens and sold eggs and milk. As the children grew older, they helped out and also went to school. Although her heroism was never publicly acknowledged, she left a legacy of what were said to be model children.[1] Children, such as hers, were often the ones to form organizations concerned with preserving cultural traditions that their mothers had taught them.

Today, upper Kittitas County, where Roslyn is located, selects a queen to reign over an annual festival that celebrates the region's ethnic diversity. The queen is an older woman, chosen each year from a different ethnic group, and is honored for her legacy and for her contributions to the community.

Environmental Preservation

"It seems to many, perhaps, an unnecessary precaution to sound the note of alarm regarding the destruction of trees by forest fires and the lumberman's ax when our Evergreen state is so richly endowed with magnificent forests, but now is the time to urge a systematic study of the trees, the influence of forests upon climatic conditions, reforestation and the proper observance of Arbor Day."[2] As newly elected president of the Washington State Federation of Women's Clubs, Elvira Marquis Elwood of Ellensburg addressed the 1902 state convention with these words, highlighting conservation as a major thrust of her administration and appointing the Spokane Floral Association to serve as the federation's initial Committee on Forestry and Outdoor Art (later renamed the Conservation Committee).

Members consulted with professors from the University of Washington and from Washington State College to study the subject and to outline a plan of action. Impressed by the WSFWC's commitment, Governor Meade appointed Elwood to the State Conservation Commission. In subsequent years, the clubs became an effective lobbying force, promoting highway beautification, preservation of natural scenery, and protection for endangered species of birds and plants. The organization gave strong support to movements to establish the Olympic National Park and to preserve the big trees along the highway to Mount Rainier.

Federation Forest

In the 1920s, under the leadership of President Esther Stark Maltby, the WSFWC launched the most ambitious conservation project in its history. She and other clubwomen had listened to the impassioned pleas of Jeanne Caithness (Greenlees), a school teacher and a member of the Everett Book Club. Caithness was a transplant from tree-shorn Wisconsin, where she had witnessed the demise of majestic forests. Fearing that the

same fate could befall her new state, she urged the WSFWC to be "park-minded" and to set an example by preserving one of the few remaining accessible stands of virgin timber for a state park.

The federation negotiated with the Snoqualmie Falls Lumber Company, a Weyerhaeuser subsidiary, to arrange purchase of a 62-acre tract along the highway on the western slope of Snoqualmie Pass. Sporting "Save a Tree" buttons, members canvassed their communities to raise funds. When "sold" for $100, a tree would be marked with a metal commemorative plate, engraved according to the wishes of the purchaser. Contributions came from individuals and organizations far and wide. The State Federation of Colored Women's Clubs proudly purchased a tree, while the National Geographic Society signaled its support with a check for $1,000.

In 1928, president Serena Matthews of Pullman presented a check for the full agreed-upon payment to the Snoqualmie Falls Lumber Company Lumber Company. She then transferred the deed for the new park to the state as a gift from the WSFWC.

In subsequent years, logging operations on adjacent lands left the park unprotected. Strong winds toppled several of the giant fir trees. To make matters worse, the highway department worried about peril to motorists and wanted to clearcut a 200-foot swath through the park on each side of the highway. As a result, the federation and the State Parks Commission asked the legislature to sell the property and use the purchase price for another tract in a more protected area.

In 1941, the new Federation Park, augmented by additional lands bought with state funds, totaled almost 600 acres. Located 15 miles east of Enumclaw on the Naches Highway, it reaches toward the Mather Memorial Parkway, a national preserve one mile wide and 50 miles long that frames the highway to Chinook Pass. The parkway was created in honor of Stephen T. Mather, an esteemed conservationist, who years before had planted a seed with the WSFWC by presenting Jeanne Caithness with the first $500 donation for a sylvan park.

During World War II, when lumber was at a premium, the park provided a model for long-range forest management with cooperation among business, government and the public. The emphasis was on cleaning up logged-off areas, reforestation, and keeping natural scenery in tact, especially along the highway. Esther Maltby later wrote, "Probably these big businessmen would scorn to admit it, but I know some clubwomen who down in the secret depths of their hearts believe that *our* project had some influence in bringing this fine plan into being."[3]

"The Botany Bunch." With their campsite surrounded by sheets of paper, these women study the flora on Mt. Baker. 1908.
Photo by Asahel Curtis. (Courtesy of the Washington State Historical Society, Tacoma, A. Curtis Photo #10770–71)

In 1890, Fay Fuller joined a party of men to become the first woman to climb Mt. Rainier. A Tacoma school teacher and journalist, she later posed for this photograph, wearing her immodest climbing costume of "blue flannel bloomers, heavy boy's shoes, a loose blouse and a small straw hat." (Courtesy of the Washington State Historical Society, Tacoma)

Audubon Society

Conservation efforts on the part of women's clubs did not stop with the state park. In 1916, Minnie M. Crickmore, a life-long bird watcher, called together a group of soul mates to form the Seattle Audubon Society. It affiliated with the national organization and eventually had a jurisdiction that encompassed western Washington. Like the Bird Department of the WSFWC, the Audubon Society saw protection of birds as a vital component of the ecosystem. Not only were birds an aesthetic treasure for nature lovers; they also devoured insects, protecting vegetation and agricultural crops.

Audubon Society members, for the most part women, took "nature walks" with note pads and opera glasses in hand to study and document bird life. Hazel Wolf, a leading member of the Seattle society since the 1950s, sees the bird song as an appropriate symbol for the spirit of the walks. She says, "Bird song is like a symphony. At first it's a big hullabaloo; then you hear the parts."[4]

Auduboners have lobbied for protection of endangered species from the hunter's gun and for bird and wildlife sanctuaries. Like the women's clubs, they brought bird study programs to youth groups and the public schools. While getting acquainted with their fine feathered friends, children learned to build bird houses and feeding stations.

In the late 1920s, the finely focused society dropped its membership in the Women's Legislative Council of Washington, so that it could save money to establish a bird sanctuary on Foster Island in the University of Washington Arboretum. Auduboners have since continued to advocate forcefully for bird sanctuaries and for protection of the environment.

Community Parks

Like the Seattle Audubon Society, clubwomen have brought the conservation efforts of their statewide organizations to their own communities. In 1906, Cheney's Tillicum Club learned that a city block was available. Wanting a place for trees and a pleasant playground for their children, the members presented a petition to the city fathers, offering to assume responsibility for developing a park. They then solicited donations of money, supplies and labor. With its bandstand, picnic tables, shade trees and play areas, Sutton Park created a valued community center which the Tillicum Club maintained for 30 years, after which the city took over the responsibility.

An outing at Liberty Lake. Spokane County, 1912. Photo by Frank Palmer. (Courtesy of the Eastern Washington State Historical Society, Spokane, F. Palmer Photo #L84327.2021)

Float in the Spokane Flower Festival parade, ca. 1910. (Courtesy of the Spokane Public Library, Northwest Room)

In Puyallup, the Teacup Club (forerunner of the Women's Club) played an active role in the development of Pioneer Park, the five-acre site of the original homestead which Ezra Meeker had donated to the city. In addition to picnic, play and garden areas, the park was the setting for the new Carnegie Library (also an outgrowth of Teacup Club activities) and a community hall. Members of the club founded the Fruit and Fair Association which built a pergola in the park to preserve the ivy that had covered the original Meeker home.

Garden Clubs

By the turn of the century women were taking a lead in founding the Garden Clubs of America. Originating with wealthy women in the East, who hired gardeners and landscape artists to carry out their ideas, garden clubs were at first exclusive. As they spread westward, their purpose broadened to include civic beautification and community involvement.

A member of the Tacoma Garden Club, Helen Bailey Murray won accolades for creating one of the most beautiful gardens in the nation at the Murray home, "Madera," located on Gravelly Lake. Similarly, Anna Herr Clise was famed for her orchids and roses which she propagated at the family's country place, "Willowmoor," on the east side of Lake Washington. Murray, Clise and others with prize-winning gardens frequently opened their grounds to the public and also played hostess to local, state, and national conventions of women's organizations. To further promote civic beautification, the early clubs gave away seeds, bulbs, and starter plants to mothers who did their own gardening.

In Washington communities, horticultural and floral associations sprouted like wildflowers with clubs for children and neophyte hobbyists, as well as for avid gardeners. The clubs contributed to city arboretums, with members attaching labels to trees, identifying them by both their popular and botanical names. They also donated valuable plant collections to city conservatories and public parks. Like the WSFWC, local garden clubs furthered highway beautification by planting trees and flowers. In Gig Harbor, the garden club set aside certain days each spring to spruce up the scenic route to Bremerton.

Sonora Louise Dodd at dedication of Mt. Spokane as the Father Mountain. (Courtesy of the Spokane Public Library, Northwest Room)

Many of the states' most cherished events—such as the Tulip, Daffodil, Apple-blossom, Rhododendron, and Strawberry Festivals—can trace their roots to an early garden club. An example is the Spokane Floral Association which was founded in 1896 with Josephine Brinkerhoff as president. At first, it sponsored floral shows, including annual competitions at the Spokane Interstate Fair. Its Floral Festival Parade was the forerunner of the city's annual rite of spring, the Lilac Festival.

In Puyallup, Sumner, LaConner, Mount Vernon and other Puget Sound communities, where flowers are a major economic commodity, women have always played an important part, both in business and through their clubs. Clubs have sponsored flower shows, awarding prizes for various categories of roses, dahlias, rhododendrons, asters, daffodils, tulips and more. Local winners have repeatedly distinguished themselves in national and international competitions. In 1935, Mrs. J. W. Lee won more than 100 prizes for her "Tacoma's Beauty," a salmon pink hybrid dahlia that she had taken 30 years to develop. Like the Lees' Dahlia Gardens, other local floral businesses have gained international acclaim and prosperity, thanks in part to the continuing participation of garden and floral societies.

The Mother of Father's Day

In Spokane, Martha Apgar Connor dedicated her prim, old-fashioned garden with its radiant profusion of roses to fatherhood. Her inspiration was Sonora Louise Smart Dodd who had listened to a sermon on Mother's Day that led her to think of honoring her own and other fathers. With support from the Ministerial Association, Spokane observed the first known Father's Day on June 10, 1910, the birthday of Dodd's father. The idea quickly caught fire, so that four years later Congress officially sanctioned the national holiday.

In Washington State and internationally, women and children planted trees to honor fathers, be they military or unsung heroes. The Federation of Women's Clubs and the International Fathers' Day Association, seeking a more permanent monument to commemorate the day, chose Mount Spokane which they dedicated in 1930 as "Father Mountain." Sonora Dodd participated and women and children carried festoons of Connor's flowers up the trail to the bald summit, where they released them to the wind.

The hauntingly lined face of Angeline, daughter of Chief Sealth for whom Seattle was named, evokes a sense of ancient heritage. A legend in her own time, she was a friend of many of the early pioneers and was visited by two United States presidents. Stoically, she refused to accept charity, lived in a waterfront shack and sold clams on street corners. When she died in 1896, her friends built a casket, shaped like a canoe, and buried her among the pioneers in Lakeview Cemetery. Her headstone was the gift of Seattle school children who collected pennies and dimes for its purchase. (Courtesy of Special Collections Div., Univ. of Washington Archives, Neg. #NA 1519)

Native American Heritage

Some of Washington's most dedicated preservationists have always been Native Americans who regard their tribal legends and history as the basis of their spirituality, environment, medicine, teachings, art, and family bonds. Like a stream, their heritage flows from ancient mythical generations, linking them with the present and creating a pantheistic affinity between the living and their forebears. By telling stories that they heard from their grandparents, tribal Elders perpetuate the ancient training that connects people through the power of myth and humor to a tradition of living wisely with the earth and with each other.

The eras of exploration and settlement ushered in a series of disasters for the Indian, including: fatal epidemics from previously unknown diseases; introduction of the demon rum; war; the forced moves from ancestral lands to reservations; the imperious stance of Christian churches against ancient spiritual traditions; and boarding schools that aimed to mold Indian children into clones of white people. The consequent fragmentation of many of the tribes resulted in lost stories, lost languages, lost traditions and lost history.

Mourning Dove of the Okanogans, discussed in the chapter on art, was a pioneer in the recording of ancient stories. Traditionally tribal history has remained unwritten and has been passed down orally by the Elders. Some resisted the departure from the oral tradition, but others saw it as a necessary means of preserving their past and teaching members of younger generations. Still others, such as Mourning Dove, wanted to foster cross-cultural understanding by sharing their history with the larger public.

More recently, some tribal Elders have agreed to record their stories on video-tape. Isabelle Arcasa of the Colville Confederated Tribes tells about experiences from her own long life and relates ancient tales passed down to her by her grandparents, that she in turn has kept alive for her grandchildren and great-grandchildren. In 1988, her granddaughter, Judge Anita Dupris, still sites the 98-year-old Arcasa as the primary influence in her life, saying "Granny is my textbook and I'm still trying to learn from her—trying to be more like her."

Ida Nason, the oldest living Native American woman in Kittitas County (ca. 100), gives personal accounts about how the Plateau Indians preserved significant aspects of their own heritage, while adapting to the dominant white culture. Using traditional Native American sign language as a means of enhancing her communication, she tells of the old ways, when her grandmother and other women rode horses up the hills to pick huckleberries and when the men caught salmon for the women to dry and store. She brings to life her spiritual ties to the environment and tells of the powerful role of women in her tribe.

An illustrative legend from the Plateau tribes tells of Tsagigla'la, "she who watches." Since ancient times, her face, characterized by concentric ovals that form goggle-like eyes, has maintained its vigil from a lofty post near Horsethief Lake on the Washington side of the Columbia River. Tsagigla'la had been chief at Wishram in the valley below, when Coyote (a powerful figure who through cataclismic actions created mountains and rivers to change the world and make it habitable for people) came by and asked her if she was an ogress, or if she treated people kindly. She answered that her goal was to teach them to live well and build good homes.

Coyote forewarned her that a time was coming when women would no longer lead, but so that she could continue to watch over people, he turned her into stone. Her image appears frequently in Indian carvings throughout the Columbia basin. According to one legend, a medicine man, who was guided by a mystical power, climbed up the cliff in the dead of night to paint the all-seeing eyes on the stone. They are said to have the power to answer prayers or to protect those who bring them gifts.[5]

The legend conveys the interconnectedness of human beings, the environment and the spirit world. It also depicts a powerful female figure which on a human scale has parallels in northwest Native American tribes.

In recent years, the Makah, the Yakima, the Colville, the Suquamish and other tribes have founded museums and cultural research centers to further document and preserve their heritage. The centers double as a meeting place for storytelling, pow-wows, conferences, salmon bakes, and other cultural events.

Notes

1. Serena F. Matthews. *History of the Washington State Federation of Women's Clubs,* unpub. ca. 1950, p. 47.
2. Esther Maltby, "The Federation Forest," unpub. 1953.
3. Lupis-Vukic, Ivo, "Some Observations on Roslyn, Washington—a typical Croatian/American Coal-Mining Town in the 1920s," Published in Split, Croatia, 1929. Translated by Richard L. Major, Seattle, for publication in the newspaper of the Croatian Fraternal Union of America (1970s).
4. "A Lesson from the Birds: Hazel Wolf Builds Harmony," *Pacific Search,* Vol. 13, Feb. 1979, pp. 19–20.
5. David Buerge, "River of Legends," *The Weekly,* Nov. 11, 1938, p. 31.

At her home on rural Greenlake (now a Seattle residential area), this woman aired out her hand-stitched quilts. Many such quilts, which at the time were both utilitarian and decorative, have been passed down through generations as treasured family heirlooms. (Courtesy of Special Collections Div., Univ. of Washington Libraries, Neg. #593)

Epilog

Following the surrender of the Japanese in 1945, Americans wanted more than anything to return to a normal life. Women who had "kept the home fires burning" during World War II quickly relinquished their jobs to male veterans; young couples marched to the altar in droves; suburbs blossomed with at-home wives, commuting husbands and families. Victorian domestic idealism was back in vogue and "women's place" was again ideally in the home—or so the myth goes.

In reality, women continued to enter the job market at an unprecedented rate. In the early 1950s, more than 10 million wives held paying jobs—two million more than at the peak of the wartime emergency—with married women outnumbering single women in the work force.[1] In rural areas where giant cooperatives and harvesting companies were revolutionizing the family farm, wives with diminishing chores and with a tradition of contributing to the family income began to join their urban counterparts, taking jobs in town. Married women's entry into the job market was a significant social trend that almost everyone overlooked. Sociologists bombarded mothers with blueprints for raising their children at home; television characterized the ideal family in popular series such as "Leave It to Beaver;" college women were rated a success if they left school with an "MRS degree." Whether they worked for pay or not, most women, like their forebears, humbly and freely continued to volunteer their time and energy to provide child services, nurture the arts, or care for the sick.

By the 1960s, popular women's magazines which for years had canonized the "happy homemaker" began to recognize the "trapped housewife." In 1961, President John F. Kennedy appointed a Commission on the Status of Women, chaired by Eleanor Roosevelt, which was charged with investigating alleged inequalities of women in the work force and which was emulated in each of the 50 states. The national commission presented its final report in 1963, documenting pervasive job discrimination against women in almost all parts of the country with a heightened bias against married women. Although the Civil Rights Act of 1964 included a provision that made sex discrimination illegal, it at first produced few results.

Adding fuel to the fire was Betty Friedan's 1963 blockbuster, *The Feminine Mystique,* which articulated the frustrations of suburban housewives, trapped in a web of conformity with lives limited to club meetings, cooking, cleaning, and chauffeuring.

In their established organizations and in informal "consciousness-raising groups," women began to challenge sex-based divisions of labor, power and wealth in the family, government, the church and the work place. In the 1970s, legions of married women turned their backs on volunteering in favor of a paycheck. Like telephones, mail delivery, and public transportation, our communities had grown so accustomed to humble, altruistic women's groups that people tended to take their contributions for granted. Many modern women no longer wanted to provide service without getting due recognition.

The temporary attack against volunteering was a serious blow to what has become an American infrastructure, causing government, corporations and communities to take notice. Voluntarism in the 1980s consequently has gained a new, upbeat image. The president, the governor and local mayors now hand out awards for voluntary service; corporate responsibility programs encourage employees to devote a percentage of their time to volunteering; colleges and employers give credit for "life experience" with individuals listing both their paid and voluntary work experience on résumés and applications for jobs or college entrance. Historian Wendy Kaminer says, "Service volunteering was repackaged as a strategy for career advancement for men and women—a bridge to the job market for the disadvantaged or disabled, a second career for the retiree. With the approval of the business community, volunteering was back in vogue."[2]

Although many women had never deviated from their voluntary commitments, the repackaging swelled the rosters of established service organizations while also giving rise to new ones. Whether they work for pay or primarily as volunteers, women—both married and single—today view voluntarism as an opportunity to serve, to play an active part in their communities and to extend themselves often beyond the limits of their comfort zones. In an effort to attract younger members, women's clubs and service organizations are creating challenging projects, such as substance abuse prevention programs, shelters for victims of domestic violence and job development programs for the developmentally disabled. Some view their activities strictly as a social service, while others interpret them in a larger context as a force for social change.

Throughout American history, women's voluntary activities have gone hand in hand with advocacy—a point that women's clubs themselves have often failed to acknowledge. Women's community service organizations move on from one problem to another, often drawing public attention to low visibility issues that exist within our midst. In the process of guiding victims of domestic abuse or rape through the criminal justice system, women's organizations have significantly altered prevailing attitudes toward sexual violence. Reminiscent of the early Women's Christian Temperance Union, Mothers Against Drunk Driving (MADD) is waging a vocal campaign for public safety. By lobbying for building codes that require access for the handicapped, women's organizations have been instrumental in enabling formerly dependent people to join the workforce.

As advocates of causes that they understand, women's groups have not only offered direct services; over the years, they have provided leadership for the suffrage movement, prohibition, conservation programs, child-care reforms, anti-war activism, comparable worth legislation, and the civil rights movement that pressured the federal government into launching the war on poverty of the 1960s.

While much of the above reflects a changing society, its source remains a wellspring that flows from the depths of women's heritage. Most of the agencies and institutions discussed in this book still serve Washington's communities; some have expanded; some have changed their focus; all that remain active continue to rely on volunteers. In recent years, the self-help group has emerged as the founder of several new service organizations. Examples are the Widowed Information and Consultation Service, the Older Women's League, Rape Relief, community day care centers, women's health care cooperatives, food banks, and employment networks.

To keep their fingers on the pulse of community and state concerns, contemporary women have also organized new civic-spirited associations such as Seattle's and Tacoma's CityClubs [sic] that emphasize awareness and that foster a spirit of commitment to public issues. Throughout the state, women of different ethnic groups continue to band together, providing mutual support and nurturing the special interests of their own communities. Examples are the Mexican American National Association (MANA) and the Southeast Asian Women's Alliance (SEAWA), both of which were founded in Seattle in the 1980's. In the cultural arena, modern women continue to organize theatre groups, music ensembles, art cooperatives and dance companies.

Today, as in the past, Washington women maintain their tradition of community service. Through door-to-door canvassing for charity, serving as museum docents or helping out at schools, women continue to provide examples for their children, showing them that caring and sharing can make a difference. Contemporary women frequently cite the lessons passed down to them by their mothers and grandmothers as their motivation for volunteering. They recognize that their forebears were indeed path breakers whose legacy is a more livable society.

Notes
1. William H. Chafe. *The American Woman: Her Changing Social, Economic and Political Roles, 1920–1970.* Oxford University Press, 1972, p. 56.
2. Wendy Kaminer, *Women Volunteering: the Pleasure, Pain and Politics of Unpaid Work from 1830 to the Present* (New York, 1984).

Bibliography

Andrews, Mildred. *Seattle Women: a Legacy of Community Development, 1851–1920*. Seattle: YWCA, 1984.

Armitage, Susan and Jameson, Elizabeth, eds. *The Women's West*. Norman and London: The University of Oklahoma Press, 1987.

Armitage, Susan. "Western Women: Beginning to Come into Focus," *Montana. The Magazine of Western History* (Summer, 1982), pp. 2–9.

Ballard, Adele M. "A Real Dramatic School for Seattle and Western Washington," *The Town Crier*, 7. (Jan., 1919), p. 7.

Bigelow, John, ed. *A Century of Service, 1858–1958: Washington Hospitals*. Seattle: Washington State Hospital Association, 1957.

Blair, Karen J. *The Clubwoman as Feminist: True Womanhood Redefined, 1868–1914*. New York: Holmes and Meier, 1980.

———. "The Limits of Sisterhood: the Woman's Building in Seattle," *Frontiers,* VII, No. 1 (1984).

———., ed. *Women in Pacific Northwest History: an Anthology*. Seattle: University of Washington Press, 1988.

Bowden, Angie Burt. *Early Schools of Washington Territory*. Seattle: Loman and Hanford Co., 1935.

Brown, H. D. *History of the Washington Children's Home Society*. unpublished paper. n.d.

Buerge, David. "River of Legends," *The Weekly,* (Nov. 11, 1987).

Carpenter, Cecelia Svinth. *They Walked Before: the Indians of Washington State*. Tacoma: Washington State Historical Society, 1977.

Cordova, Fred. *Filipinos: Forgotten Asian Americans*. Dubuque: Kendall/Hunt, 1983.

Cornish, Nellie. *Miss Aunt Nellie: the Autobiography of Nellie C. Cornish*. Ellen Van Volkenburg Browne and Edward Nordhoff Beck, eds. Seattle: University of Washington Press, 1964.

Drury, C. M. "The Columbia Maternal Association," *Oregon Historical Quarterly,* 39 (1938), pp. 99–122.

Duniway, Abigail Scott. *Path Breaking: an Autobiographical History of the Equal Suffrage Movement in Pacific Coast States*. New Intro. by Eleanor Flexner. New York: Schocken Books, 1971. Reprinted from James, Kerns & Abbott Edition of 1914.

Fargo, Lucille. *Spokane Story*. Minneapolis: Northwestern Press, 1957.

Fields, Ronald M. *Abby Rhoda Williams Hill, 1961–1943: Northwest Frontier Artist*. Tacoma: Washington State Historical Society, forthcoming.

Flexnor, Eleanor. *Century of Struggle: the Women's Rights Movement in the United States*. New York: Atheneum, 1970.

Franklin, Joe. "The Ku Klux Klan in the City of Spokane, 1921–1924," *Pacific Northwest Forum,* Vol. XI, No. 9 (Winter, 1986).

Goetter, Patricia S. *A History of the Inland Empire Chapter of the American Red Cross, 1881–1981*. unpublished paper. Spokane, 1981.

Greenwald, Maurine Weiner. "Working Class Feminism and the Family Wage Ideal: the Seattle Debate on Married Women's Right to Work in the Era of the First World War." *Journal of American History* (forthcoming, June, 1989).

Harris, Minnie N. "The Women Build a Museum," *Pacific Northwest Quarterly,* 43 (April, 1952) 158–169.

Hazard, Joseph T. *Pioneer Teachers of Washington*. Seattle: Retired Teachers Association, 1955.

Hinsch, Kathryn, ed. *Political Pioneers: a Study of Women in the Washington State Legislature*. Elected Washington Women, 1983.

Hum-Ishu-Ma, "Mourning Dove," *Cogewea, the Half-Blood*. Intro. by Dexter Fisher. Omaha: University of Nebraska Press, 1981.

Ito, Kazuo. *Issai*. Trans. by Shinichiro Nakamura and Jean S. Gerard. Seattle-Japanese Community Service, 1973.

Jennings, Judson T. "Histories of Libraries in Washington: the Seattle Public Library" *Library News Bulletin.* (May–June, 1941).

Larson, T. A., "The Woman Suffrage Movement in Washington," *Pacific Northwest Quarterly* (April, 1976).

Luchetti, Cathy and Olwell, Carol. *Women of the West*. Utah: Antelope Island Press, 1982.

Lucia, Ellis. *Seattle's Sisters of Providence*. Seattle: Sisters of Providence, 1978.

———. *Magic Valley: The Story of St. Joseph Academy and the Blossoming of Yakima*. Seattle: Sisters of Providence, 1976.

Lupis-Vukic, Ivo. "Some Observations on Roslyn, Washington—a Typical Croatian/American Coal-Mining Town in the 1920s." Published in Split, Croatia, 1929. Trans. by Richard L. Major, Seattle, for publication in the newspaper of the Croatian Fraternal Union of America (1970s).

Maltby, Esther. "The Federation Forest." unpublished paper. 1953.

Marr, Carolyn, ed. *Portrait in Time: Photos of the Makah by Samuel G. Morse, 1896–1903,* The Makah Cultural and Research Center and the Washington State Historical Society, 1987.

Matthews, Serena F. *History of the Washington State Federation of Women's Clubs*. unpublished paper, ca. 1950.

McDonald, Lucille and Richard K. *The Coals of Newcastle*. Issaquah: Issaquah Alps Trails Club, 1987.

Montgomery, James W. *Liberated Woman: a Life of May Arkwright Hutton*. Spokane: Gingko House Publishers, 1974.

Morgan, Murray. *Puget's Sound: Narrative of Early Tacoma and South Sound*. Seattle and London: University of Washington Press, 1979.

Monihan, Ruth Barnes. *Rebel for Rights: Abigail Scott Duniway*. New Haven and London: Yale University Press, 1983.

Mumford, Esther Hall. *Seattle's Black Victorians, 1852–1901*. Seattle: Ananse Press, 1980.

——. *Seven Stars & Orion: Reflections of the Past*. Seattle: Ananse Press, 1986.

Otis, Emma. *Historical Record of Girl Scouting in Pierce County*. unpublished paper. Tacoma, 1962.

Petrik, Paula. *No Step Backward*. Helena: Montana Historical Society, 1987.

Radcliffe, W. O. E. *Fifty Golden Years: a History of the Washington Congress of Parents and Teachers, 1905–1955*. Seattle Printing and Publishing Co., 1955.

Schwabacher, Emilie. *A Place for the Children*. Seattle: Children's Orthopedic Hospital, 1977.

Smith, Catherine Parsons and Richardson, Cynthia S. *Mary Carr Moore: American Composer*. Ann Arbor: University of Michigan Press, 1987.

Smith, Charles W. "Early Library Development in Washington," *Washington Historical Quarterly*, 17. (1926).

Tsutakawa, Mayumi, ed. *Turning Shadows into Light*. Seattle: Young Pine Press, 1982.

Turner, Russell M. *The First 45 Years: a History of Cooperative Extension in Washington State*. Pullman: Washington State University Extension Miscellaneous Publication 55, 1961.

Warren, James R. *King County and Its Queen City: Seattle*. California: Windsor Publications, 1981.

Whitney, Marci. *Notable Women*. Tacoma: *Tacoma News Tribune,* 1977.

Note: Numerous additional sources were consulted including regional periodicals and archives. Of special value were interviews with individuals and unpublished records, such as diaries, correspondence, club minutes and scrapbooks.

Index